THE CONSCIENTIOUS OBJECTOR

AND THE

UNITED STATES ARMED FORCES

Daniel H. Shubin

PEACE CHURCH CHALLENGE
Bakersfield, CA

Revised January 5, 2008
Copyright 2008
Daniel H. Shubin

ISBN: 978-0615-26168-3

Peace Church Challenge
Email: peacechurch@jps.net
Web site: www.peacehost.net/peacechurch

FORWARD

This book is a compendium of the attitude of the United States Armed Forces toward the conscientious objector (C.O.). It includes the portions of US military and Selective Service regulations that deal with the C.O. Included is the procedure for the C.O. to acquire a release from military service and what he should expect in the process. Also in case of a future conscription, the procedure to acquire an exemption as a C.O. is provided along with the requirement of alternative service. Also provided are a sample copy of the US Army and Selective Service forms that deal with acquiring an exemption or discharge from military service.

BIBLIOGRAPHY

This book is not complete, but will be supplemented as required as requirements for compulsory military service or training are legislated by the US Congress and as rules are issued by the various branches of the Armed Forces or the Selective Service System.

The following documents and publication have been utilized in the creation of this book:

US Code Title 50, Appendices 451-473
    The Military Selective Service Act
32 CFR XVI, Part 1636
    Selective Service Regulations
Department of Defense Form 4/1
    Enlistment Contract
Department of Defense Directive 1300.6
    Conscientious Objectors
Department of Defense Directive 1322.14
    Enlisted Administrative Separations
Army Regulation 600-43
    Conscientious Objection
Army Regulation 635-200
    Personnel Separations
Army Regulation 601-95
    Delayed Entry Program

Army Regulation 601-56
        Delayed Entry Program Separation
Army Regulation 601-210
        Army Enlistment Program

Helping Out: A Guide to Military Discharges, by Alex Doty of the CCCO.
Advice for C.O.s in the Armed Forces, by Robert Seeley of the CCCO
The Draft Counselor's Manual by Bill Galvin and J.E. McNeil of NISBCO.

Although this book is written in terms of the C.O. being a Christian, it can be equally applied to a person of any religion, or no religion, using the same premise for beliefs and the use of other religious texts. According to Selective Service Regulations, an atheist person can also be a C.O. provided that his convictions have an impact on his beliefs in the same manner as would a supreme being.

More information on the Christian basis of conscientious objection to war and military service is available on the following web sites:

www.christianpacifism.com

www.peacehost.net/peacechurch

This book is written in the male gender, since the majority of recruits are male, but also applies equally and in all respects to the female.

TABLE OF CONTENTS

PART 1

INTRODUCTION

1.1 Purpose of this Book

This book is a compilation of procedures and related information on the relationship between the conscientious objector (C.O.), and the United States military and Selective Service System (SSS), and can be used for the following purposes:

1. To provide information to relate to a young person regarding the option of exemption to military service as a conscientious objector.
2. To assist a C.O. with acquiring an exemption from conscription or from the military portion of National Service, should it be legislated.
3. To assist a young person who has enlisted for military service and seeks discharge as a conscientious objector.

After the Kuwaiti War in 1991 by order of the president at the time the entire US Armed Forces began renovation. Regulations and policies were rewritten. Those policies in effect during Viet-Nam and earlier were essentially discarded and became obsolete. These procedures incorporate the most recent information published by the military. As time progresses more rules will be issued and this information will be acquired from the Selective Service System and other C.O. organizations, and these sections will be added to this book.

1.2 Present State of the US Armed Forces

The US military possesses about 1.4 million active personnel, and has about 1.2 million reservists available. The present rate of voluntary recruitment is about 120,000 per year, of which about 80,000 is the US Army, and the balance divided up among the Navy, Air Force and Marines. In 1975, by order of President Gerald Ford at the end of Viet-Nam War, the Selective Service System was dismantled, registration was cancelled and all classifications terminated. Essentially the SSS went dormant. In 1980 by order of President Jimmy Carter only registration for draft was legislated. The SSS presently remains active in registration and operates on a budget of $28 million.

At present, the intent of the President, the Pentagon and the US Congress is a complete volunteer army. No conscription will begin until Congress amends the Military Selective Service Act to restore to the President the power to begin inductions, and conscription is legislated. Congress must also fund about $500 million to the Selective Service System, which is the cost of conscription, and hire about 13,000 additional personnel to staff offices throughout the USA.

Once the law goes into effect the Selective Service System has 193 days to provide the first recruits to military bases. During this interval the SSS must establish country-wide draft boards, supply them with personal, and introduce a massive bureaucracy and communication network, all of which is expensive and time-consuming. Conscription also has a negative effect on the morale of soldiers and on military campaigns. The lesson learned by military officials from Viet-Nam era conscription is that a volunteer army is the most effective because it is against the natural will of a conscript – a person forced into military service against his wishes – for him to either give his life for his country or kill for his country.

1.3 Advisors of Recruits who are C.O.

It is never too late to be discharged from the military. The primary role of a C.O. Advisor is to advise young persons regarding the option of being a C.O. due to their moral and religious convictions. The greater responsibility for an Advisor will be to assist the young person who wants discharge from the military after they have enlisted, now realizing that they are conscientious objectors.

The only person that can get a recruit discharged is themselves. They got themselves into the military and they are the only one that can get themselves out. An Advisor's responsibility is to inform the recruit of the means and route that must be taken within the bureaucracy of the US Armed Forces to acquire a discharge. An Advisor must walk them through the channels, assist them in filling out forms and writing letters, and appear with them at administrative hearings in front of military administrative boards. More than all, an Advisor must support the decision of the recruit seeking discharge, and make sure his parents, relatives and elders support him. The recruit may be harassed and intimidated for wanting a discharge and even spend time in incarceration pending resolution of his request. They should be supported in order for them not to give up until finally acquiring a discharge.

1.4 Draft Registration

Under a Presidential proclamation in 1980, all males age 18 through 26 must register with the Selective Service system for a potential draft for military service. You can register at any U.S. post office or at a consular office in another country. The official registration period is 60 days, beginning 30 days before the eighteenth anniversary of your birth. Aliens who are permanent residents, or who have work permits, must also register. Foreign students, dependents of members of the diplomatic corps, and visitors do not have to register. Aliens must register within 30 days of entry into the U.S. During the first year of their residence in the U.S., aliens are not subject to the draft.

To register, you must fill out a card giving your name, social security number (if you have one), current address, permanent address and phone number. Write somewhere on the form: **I am a conscientious objector to war in any form**, before mailing it. Make and keep a copy of the form for your personal records.

1.5 Discharge or Separation?

A discharge completely cuts off all legal ties a person has to the military. Separation is a more general term which includes discharge, release from active duty, transfer to the inactive reserves, and similar changes in active or reserve status. For example, if an application for a discharge is approved, the recruit will be discharged with no possibility of being called for active duty. However, if the recruit was given an early release for a hardship in your family or for pregnancy, they would be separated, but not necessarily discharged. Many separations result in a transfer to the inactive reserves also known as the Individual Ready Reserve (IRR) for the rest of the term of enlistment and they are still eligible for call–up in a mobilization.

Under no conditions should the recruit agree to transfer to IRR, since they will still be liable to mobilization in case of war or national emergency through the end of their 8-year term of enlistment.

1.6 Vocation of the Soldier

The vocation of a soldier is to kill the enemy, whether with a knife or bayonet, gun or rifle or machine gun, shooting a missile or dropping a bomb. The soldier fulfills his obligation when he kills or destroys property belonging to the enemy in a foreign land. Wars are won only by killing more of the enemy and destroying more of their property, than they destroy of you and your property. Wars are fought to be won, not to be lost. A soldier is not in the military to give his life for his country, but to make sure that the enemy gives up his life for his country and as many that he can without losing his own life in the process. Others that are members of the military have the responsibility to assist the soldier in performing his task, whether giving him orders, supplying him with weapons or equipment necessary to perform this task, tending to his wounds if he is wounded, or by comforting and encouraging him when he loses courage. Whether combatant or non-combatant they are all employees of the military killing industry.

Because depriving another person of their life is against the grain of human nature every recruit must be trained to kill and be able to do so on command by his officer without affecting his conscience. This is the reason for the military to require every recruit to successfully pass boot camp training, in order to change or obliterate the inherent nature of that person. Because the God-given nature of every person is not to kill, injure or maim or destroy property, in order to fight and win wars the military must alter that God-given nature through indoctrination, training in the use and performance of weapons, and through simulated techniques of killing.

This book is written in the male gender, since the majority of recruits are male, but also applies equally and in all respects to the female.

Penalties for any failure to comply with duties defined in Selective Service regulations are up to 5 years imprisonment and fines up to $250,000 during wartime (Military Selective Service Act, Sec. 462(a)). Failure to appear for induction or refusal of induction has a penalty of up to 5 years imprisonment and $10,000 or both. (AR 601-270, Sec 9-40).

In peacetime, with registration only, the regular maximum penalties are 4 months and/or $2500. The Selective Service does not use draft registration to track military age Americans, but DMV records, and military recruiters have access to high school records of all students. Not registering for the draft will only make it more difficult to acquire an exemption if conscription or National Service is legislated.

PART 2

THE MILITARY AND THE CONSCIENTIOUS OBJECTOR

2.1 Definition of a Conscientious Objector

The basis to allow discharge or exemption from military service of a C.O. is found in the following passage of the Military Selective Service Act, USC title 50, Appendix 456 (j):

> Nothing contained in this title [sections 451 to 471a of this Appendix] shall be construed to require any person to be subject to combatant training and service in the armed forces of the United States who, by reason of religious training and belief, is conscientiously opposed to participation in war in any form. As used in this subsection, the term "religious training and belief" does not include essentially political, sociological, or philosophical views, or a merely personal moral code.

The Selective Service regulations (32 CFR XVI) state the following:

> Sec. 1636.4 Basis for classification in Class 1-0.
> (a) A registrant must be conscientiously opposed to participation in war in any form and conscientiously opposed to participation in both combatant and noncombatant training and service in the Armed Forces.
> (b) A registrant's objection may be founded on religious training and belief; it may be based on strictly religious beliefs, or on personal beliefs that are purely ethical or moral in source or content and occupy in the life of a registrant a place parallel to that filled by belief in a Supreme Being for those holding more traditionally religious views.
> (c) A registrant's objection must be sincere.

DOD 1300.6 defines a C.O. in the following terms:

> 3.1. Conscientious Objection: General - A firm, fixed and sincere objection to participation in war in any form or the bearing of arms, by reason of religious training and belief.
> 3.1.1. Class 1-O Conscientious Objector. A member who, by reason of conscientious objection, sincerely objects to participation of any kind in war in any form.

DOD 1300.6 also defines what religious training and belief consist of.

> 3.2. Religious Training and Belief: Belief in an external power or being or deeply held moral or ethical belief, to which all else is subordinate or upon which all else is ultimately dependent, and which has the power or force to affect moral-well-being. The external power or being need not be of an orthodox deity, but may be a sincere and meaningful belief which occupies in the life of its possessor a place parallel to that filled by the God of another, or, in the case of deeply held moral or ethical beliefs, a belief held with the strength and devotion of traditional religious conviction. The term "religious training and belief" may include solely moral or ethical beliefs even though the applicant himself may not characterize these beliefs as "'religious" in the traditional sense, or may expressly characterize them as not religious. The term "religious training and belief" does not include a belief which rests solely upon considerations of policy, pragmatism, expediency, or political views.

It is important to note that political, economic or humanitarian reasons are insufficient as a claim of conscientious objection to war and military service. **The exemption is aligned with the First Amendment statement of freedom of religion.** The state cannot force a person to violate his proven religious convictions. All conscientious objection claims must be associated with religious beliefs or equally-valid convictions resulting from a divine authority above that of the state. An atheist can also be a C.O. provided that he can prove that his convictions have the same impact on his life as would belief in a supreme being.

Note the following Selective Service qualifier regarding exclusions from a C.O. exemption (32 CFR XVI, Sec. 1636.5):

A registrant shall be excluded from Class 1-A-0 or Class 1-0:

(a) Who asserts beliefs which are of a religious, moral or ethical nature, but who is found not to be sincere in his assertions; or

(b) Whose stated objection to participation in war does not rest at all upon moral, ethical, or religious principle, but instead rests solely upon considerations of policy, pragmatism, expediency, or his own self-interest or well-being; or

(c) Whose objection to participation in war is directed against a particular war rather than against war in any form (a selective objection). If a registrant objects to war in any form, but also believes in a theocratic, spiritual war between the forces of good and evil, he may not by reason of that belief alone be considered a selective conscientious objector.

2.2   The Military Recruiter and the Conscientious Objector

According to Army Regulation 601-210, paragraph 4-1, any person who professes conscientious objection or religious convictions that oppose military service cannot enlist.

The military does not want to recruit any person that may possibly refuse to honor their obligation to be a soldier for the balance of the 8 year term of enlistment. They are well aware of the difficulties that can occur if a person having inclination toward C.O. is recruited. As a result of this to weed out any person who may fail as a soldier due to C.O. convictions the preliminary enlistment questionnaire has 3 questions for the US Marine Corp, and similar for the other branches of the service, that a candidate for recruitment must answer "No" in order to be allowed to join:

1. Do you have any personal convictions that would preclude you from performing as a soldier during the term of your enlistment?

2. Do you have any convictions or beliefs as a conscientious objector?

3. Have you had any religious training in the area of conscientious objection that would prohibit you from fulfilling your role as a soldier?

If the possible recruit should answer "Yes" to any of the above 3 questions he will be denied enlistment. In addition to the above preliminary enlistment questionnaire, the recruit must also sign AR (Army) Form 3286, Statements for Enlistment, or the form applicable to that branch of the Armed Forces they are joining, which includes the following paragraph:

> k. I am not conscientiously opposed by reason of religious training or belief to bearing arms or to participation or training for war in any form.

It is very difficult after induction and once training begins for a recruit to acquire discharge as a C.O., because he has already admitted that he is not a C.O. by answering "No" to the above questions in the preliminary enlistment questionnaire and signing AR Form 3286. In the year 2002, only 29 recruits were granted a discharge after completion of basic training due to C.O. of the 1.5 million active military personnel. During the proceedings all of them endured extreme physical and psychological hardship by military commanders who attempted to steer them away from discharge and the process took an average of 12 months.

PART 3

MILITARY RECRUITMENT

3.1 Military Commitment

The commitment of a recruit is for 8 years during peacetime: from 2 to 4 years is in active service (depending on the branch of the service and the recruitment officer), while the balance is as an Armed Forces Reservist. A term of 3 years of active service is required to acquire any benefits. In case of war or national emergency, the term of active service is automatically extended to 10 years and possibly an additional 6 months. Congress can also legislate peace-time conscription if the number of armed forces personnel falls below some point that national security is jeopardized. This point is defined by the Pentagon. The minimum age of recruitment is 18, unless the parents are willing to sign for their son or daughter who is age 17. It is illegal for the military to recruit any younger than age 17.

The reservists are automatically first to be returned to active service in case of national emergency or war if insufficient active personnel are available. Now the obligation of the reservist in active service is for 24 months or to the end of their term of enlistment plus an additional 6 months if required to complete 24 months. During their term as a reservist the obligation is 1 week-end a month plus 2 weeks per year continuous training, plus they receive a check from the military every month depending on their rank and service.

If a reservist is called for active service they will loose their regular job income and return to military pay. Unless the recruit is independently wealthy their family will have to acquire government assistance. (This is the dilemma of many in Iraq at present.)

3.2 Effort of Military Recruiters

Military Recruiters are under pressure to recruit, which is cheaper than a draft. They are provided with special privileges and tools to present the military in the best possible light to culpable high schools students, emphasizing benefits on completion. The recruiters are paid bonuses and acquire special benefits based on the number of recruits they can round up and they have a quota to meet, but in order to perform their job they do not tell the complete truth about the military, that its primary purpose is the train them as soldiers to kill and destroy, and that a recruit is the property of the state. The military videos and advertisements glorify the benefits, but they don't show the dead on the battlefield or the soldier in boot camp. Some recruiters even have a trailer with a simulated jet fighter cockpit and controls for students to try out and shoot down an enemy aircraft, much like a video game.

The target of the recruiters are recent high school graduates who have no plans for the future. Those especially susceptible to recruitment are persons from a broken home, or those from lower income families or lower economic groups of society. They see the military are a means of advancement in both prestige and promise of a future.

Recruiters enlist about 80,000 new recruits per year just for the army, with a total of about 120,000 per year for the entire US military. It costs the American taxpayer about $16,000 for every person that is recruited into the military. In 2003, $4 billion was spent by military recruiters to recruit and re-enlist the 250,000 persons, which includes reservists and re-enlistments.

It is important to remember that a person is not officially in the military until they actually appear for induction at a Military Entrance Processing Station (MEPS) and are processed. Even though enlistment papers may be voluntarily signed, a recruit can refuse to be inducted without criminal consequences or prosecution up to the point that induction is completed. This will be further discussed. Under a military draft, it will be very difficult if a person waits that long before deciding that he is a conscientious objector. The military does not treat traitors lightly.

3.3 Military Recruiters and High School Students

On January 8, 2002 , President George Bush signed a Federal education bill which went into effect as Public Law 107-110 on May 8, 2002 . One section of this education bill allows military recruiters access to the name, address and phone number of all high school students in 11th and 12th grades.

Military recruiters are under pressure to recruit, especially at the present with the Pentagon, Congress, and President in favor of a volunteer army. With the name as address and phone number of your high school young adult, they have the legal right to contact them to present them with the opportunity to join the military. Military recruiters are provided with special privileges and tools to present the military in the best possible light to culpable high school students. The recruiters are paid bonuses and themselves acquire special benefits based on the number of recruits they can round up, and they do have a quota to meet. But in order to meet their quota they do not tell the complete truth about military service, that its primary purpose is to turn them into killing machines. The recruiters emphasize paid schooling and large discharge bonuses upon completion of a 4-year active duty assignment. What they do not tell the students, is their assignment to some battlefield, up to 6 years in active service, and for a total of 8 years minimum obligatory military service, and longer in wartime, as at present.

Legally, parents have the right to stop the release of their children's personal information to Armed Forces recruiters.

The same education bill contains a provision that allows parents to inform their school district, that they do not want the school district to release this information to military recruiters. This is usually a form that is attached to other forms and is mailed to the parents, or that the student takes home with them. Sometimes, the statement is nothing more than a sentence or 2 that is buried in the context of other school information. The information is provided to the parents at the beginning of the school year, for both junior and senior high school students.

If you do not want your child's personal information to be released to Armed Forces recruiters, then you must find the form in the package of information from your child's high school, and fill out the form, and tell them NOT to release your child's personal information to the military. If there is no form, then, the parent must write a personal letter to the high school principal, telling them NOT to release your child's name, address or phone number to military recruiters. The student also has the right to write his own letter. This must be done at the beginning of each junior and senior high school year for each student. If you do not have a child in high school, please pass this letter on to someone you know who has, or nephew or niece or grandchild.

3.4 The Montgomery G.I. Bill

The present G.I. Bill should not be confused with the G.I. Bill of previous generations. This bill solely provides scholarship and pre-paid education funds. For the recruit to enter the Montgomery G.I. Bill program, $100 per month is taken out of his military pay for the initial 12 months of his service, a total of $1200. To quality for benefits the recruit must have an honorable discharge from the service with at least 3 years of active duty, the G.I. Bill will then pay for education with a maximum amount about $36,000. This number is a deception because the plan only pays for tuition and textbooks and direct school expenses at community and state colleges and universities. The plan does not pay for any private schools. (The idea is for the money to go back into circulation of the local or state government and not into the hands of private schools.)

Only 42% of all veterans take advantage of any of the plan, and only 20% actually enter a 4-year college or university. A quarter of them eventually drop out, meaning that only 15% of veterans that enter college will complete a 4-year degree. The experience of those seeking higher education in 4-year universities is disappointing because of the short term of benefits, many finding it difficult to further their education with a family to also support. Of the 42% of veterans that do return to school, only 70% of them actually have expenses beyond $1200, since most will attend a local community college. One key weakness of the MGIB is that any other financial aid programs that you quality for will deduct money received from the government. So the overall help is minimal. In summary, young recruits are deceiving themselves, thinking they will actually acquire a 4-year degree upon discharge from the military, now that they are 4 years older, and often with some battle scar, either physical or psychological.

3.5 The Dilemma of the Recruit

The recruit will never advance in the military unless he decides to become a career soldier. Since active service is only 2 or 4 years the military is hardly planning to invest any more than the minimum necessary into their training and education. The vocational training provided in the military is the absolute minimum for the soldier to perform his duty, and in the majority of cases this training is not applicable in the civilian world because military equipment and method of operation is very different than that of civilian equipment. If a recruit re-enlists only then will more opportunity be offered him to advance in education and training.

A typical recruit will never become an officer, because officers are selected from the following: college graduates in military or political oriented curriculum; Reserve Officers Training Corp (ROTC) graduates; military school graduates (West Point, etc.). These enter the military directly as a non-commissioned officer and the military views them as career personnel who plan to retire from the military.

3.6 Medical Fitness

Subsequent to induction all candidates for recruitment will have a physical examination performed on them. This normally occurs at the Military Entrance Processing Station (MEPS) at the same time the ASVAB test is given. Figure 9-5 of Army Regulation 601-270 is a list of disqualifying medical conditions for military service.

3.7 JROTC

Junior Reserve Officers Training Corps is a program run by the US Department of Defense. This program is used to promote good public relations in high schools for the military. JROTC instructors are retired military personnel with minimal training as educators. All facets of JROTC programs are exempt from local school board review. The overall purpose of JROTC is to introduce military regimentation and education to high school students. The success rate of the JROTC is immense, about 70% of all graduates of JROTC programs enter the military.

PART 4

ARMED SERVICES VOCATIONAL APTITUDE BATTERY

4.1 What is ASVAB?

All persons enlisting in the US military are required to take the Armed Services Vocational Aptitude Battery (ASVAB). It is a test that determines whether a potential recruit is qualified for the military and if he is qualified, then what military job would they be best suited for. Unlike the army of previous generations the contemporary military wants "smart" recruits and this test allows recruitment officers the ability to concentrate on talented persons that the military could utilize.

The ASVAB is a three-hour test that consists of 10 sections: Word Knowledge; Paragraph Comprehension; Arithmetic Reasoning; Mathematics Knowledge; General Science; Auto and Shop Information; Mechanical Comprehension; Electronics Information; Numerical Operations; and Coding Speed. The ASVAB is supposed to look for talent and natural skills in subject areas that are considered important for different military jobs. The ASVAB is not an IQ test: it does not measure intelligence. The test was designed specifically to measure an individual's aptitude to be trained in specific jobs.

4.2 High School ASVAB

In the 1960s, Department of Defense decided to develop a standardized military selection & classification test, and administer it throughout U.S. High schools. Armed Services Vocational Aptitude Battery (ASVAB) tests were first used in high schools in 1968, but it wasn't used for military recruiting until a few years later.

The ASVAB is voluntary and offered to 10th, 11th and 12th graders in high school, to both male and female. The test is administered at more than 13,000 high schools in the United States and approximately 900,000 students take the test each year. There is no need for any parental consent for the student to take the test.

Do not allow your high school student to take this test if the school he or she attends is offering it. Just remember, there is no law that requires a student to take this test or to talk to recruiters.

Military recruiters use ASVAB to target recruitment of young people while still in high school. Recruiters advertise the test to students as a means to determine their vocational aptitude in general whether they join the military or not. However recruitment officers correlate their scores to the high school student's chance of success in the military and of course everyone passes.

ASVAB is one way recruiters get personal information about students. Typically recruiters obtain contact information (such as name, address, phone number, courses taken, and extracurricular activities) from the school administration or district office, but the ASVAB gives them much more personal information about potential recruits. Recruiters give special attention to students in the 11th or 12th grade who meet minimum standards – what they refer to as "pre-qualified leads." They use test information (scores, name, address, etc.) to identify and reach young people they hope to enlist. Recruiters contact these young people by letters, phone calls, and visits to home and school. Students may receive calls from recruiters even if they say they are not interested in joining the military. One often-used tactic is to leave a message for a student telling them of an appointment with a recruiter, even if the student didn't ask for one.

4.3 The Recruit and ASVAB

After enlistment or after conscription, the recruit will take the enlistment ASVAB to determine their best use by the branch of service they are joining. The test will be taken at the Military Entrance Processing Station (MEPS) at the same time they are given a physical. After passing both physical and obtaining a successful or passing score on the ASVAB the recruit will be inducted and recite his oath of allegiance.

If a person attempts to deliberately fail the test to avoid conscription they will be inducted regardless. Emphasis is placed on the fact that a deliberate attempt to fail aptitude tests will not keep a person out of military service; that person will be inducted regardless of their score if they are found not trying to do their best and otherwise could have passed (Army Regulation 601-270, par. 9-33).

PART 5

RELEASE FROM THE DELAYED ENTRY PROGRAM

5.1 What is the DEP?

The Delayed Entry Program (DEP) allows a person to join a branch of the military up to a year before they report for active duty training. Many young people sign up in their last year of high school and then finish school before starting military service. Some sign up at age 17 and delay enlistment until their 18th birthday. The maximum length of delay is one year. This is also a recruitment tactic. *Remember that a recruit is not officially in the military until he actually appears at a Military Entrance Processing Station (MEPS) and completes induction.* The process for discharge while under the DEP is simple compared to if the person has completed induction and is already at boot camp.

The regulation that deals with DEP is Army 601-95, while the regulation that deals with release from DEP is Army 601-56. The regulations of other branches are similar.

5.2 Release from the DEP

The average rate of release from DEP is 15% to 24% depending on the specific branch of service, and it is not difficult.

The recruit must write a letter to the commander of the recruitment office that they signed up at. This information is available on the enlistment documents. If the name of the commander is not known just address the letter to Commanding Officer and send a copy of the letter to the recruitment officer. Send all letters certified with return receipt. The letter must be specific as to the reason why the recruit requests a release and does not want to join the service, and just about any sincere and concrete reason is sufficient. An example of reasons are the following:

- You have signed up at a college or vocational school to further your education instead.

- You have accepted a new job that has a secure future.
- A recent marriage had forced you to decide otherwise with your life due to new responsibilities
- You have recently acquired religious convictions of opposition to war and military service (conscientious objection), and cannot proceed any further.
- Your wife is – or you if you are female are – pregnant.
- A latent medical condition has surfaced, which will preclude your performance in the military.
- Personal or psychological problems have developed since enlistment.
- A sudden hardship on the family has arisen due to death of a family member that requires you to become sole supporter.
- An appointment as a minister.
- Your complete misunderstanding of the enlistment process, meaning you did not understand the obligation as a soldier in the military and what is expected of you in war.

State in the letter that for the above reason or reasons you are unable to join the service and request a release from DEP and separation from the military. Include your Social Security number and sign it. Send the letter to the recruiting office and to the commander in charge, or even deliver the letter in person, so there is no mistake with them receiving it.

Appendix F of Army Regulation 601-56 requires documentation to substantiate the claim of the recruit wanting a release, such as a letter from a doctor in case of pregnancy or some medical condition, a marriage certificate in case of marriage, or a letter from the school you have been admitted to. However in case of a new job, personal problems, hardship or conscientious objection, only a statement to that effect is required in the body of the letter as evidence. The minister of your church can also write a letter to provide evidence that you have acquired convictions of religious objection to war and military service since your enlistment.

5.3 Response of the Recruitment Office

The recruiter will call and try to convince you to reconsider. The recruitment officer may threaten you telling you that you cannot be released, that what you are doing is a violation of the Uniform Code of

Military Justice (UCJM), that you will be arrested, that this will affect your criminal record and keep you from getting a job or furthering your education. However, all such threats by the recruiting officer are false and illegal. According to Army Regulation 601-56:

> Member of the recruiting force must respond positively to any inquiry from DEP members concerning separations from the DEP. Under no circumstances will any member of this command threaten, coerce, manipulate or intimidate DEP members, nor may they obstruct separation requests.
>
> When such an inquiry is received, local recruiting personnel will attempt to resell the DEP member on an Army enlistment. (3-1(c)).

The recruit must ignore all requests from the recruitment officer to convince them to change their mind and must ignore all threats and hold to their request for release.

The recruitment office will send to you form Fm 986 (See copy Appendix XVI) or the form applicable to that branch of the service. The form will be filled out by the recruit and signed and returned to the recruitment office or address that is requested. Please keep a copy of all letters and forms.

Even after signing and submitting Fm 986 the recruitment officer has the right (Army Regulation 601-56 par. 3-2(c)), to call regularly to convince the recruit to change their mind, but only to a maximum length of one year. DO NOT GIVE IN !!!

If the recruitment office delays in response to the request and orders are delivered to you for induction at MEPS, do not go. Call the recruitment office and inform the recruitment officer of the situation and deliver another copy of the same letter to the commander at the recruitment office. Ask for an extension of your DEP until the matter is resolved.

You are not officially released from the DEP and separated from the military until you receive in the mail a signed copy of Army Fm 500 or the form applicable to that branch of the service (See sample copy Appendix XVII).

PART 6

ENTRY LEVEL SEPARATION

6.1 What is Entry Level Separation (ELS)?

The military term is **Entry Level Performance and Conduct Discharge.** If a recruit is in entry level status and cannot adjust socially or emotionally to military life or cannot meet the minimum standards of the training program, they are eligible for separation. Entry level status is the first 180 days of active duty. The military is hesitant to allow discharge to recruits without solid reason to do so. In addition to the cost of $9600 per recruit noted above for recruitment expense, it costs the American taxpayer an additional $35,000 for the 6 months of boot camp training of every recruit.

According to Department of Defense (DoD) regulation 1332.14:

> E3.A1.1.1.6.1.1 A member may be separated while in entry level status when it is determined under the guidance in section E3.A2.1.1 of Part 2, that the member is unqualified for further military service by reason of unsatisfactory performance or conduct (or both) as evidenced by inability, lack of reasonable effort, failure to adapt to the military environment, or minor disciplinary infractions.

Par. E3.A2.1.1 of Part 2 requires that reasonable effort of rehabilitation of the recruit requesting ELS must be performed by the military, and only after rehabilitation is attempted and failed will proceedings begin for ELS.

Also according to Army Regulation 635-200:

> The Army makes a substantial investment in training, time, equipment and related expenses when persons enter into military service. Separation prior to completion of an obligated period of service is wasteful because it results in loss of this investment and generates a requirement for increased accessions. Consequently, attrition is an issue of significant concern at all levels of responsibility within the Army (1-1.c.3)

Reasonable efforts should be made to identify soldiers who exhibit likelihood for early separation and to improve their chances for retention through counseling, retraining, and rehabilitation prior to initiation of separation proceedings. (1-1.c.3.a)

Soldiers who do not conform to required standards of discipline and performance and soldiers who do not demonstrate potential for further military service should be separated in order to avoid the high costs in terms of pay, administrative efforts, degradation of morale, and substandard mission performance. (1-1.c.3.b)

The attrition rate in the military is immense. About 20% of the men and 18% of the women leave the military before the end of their initial enlistment. Many of them are discharged due to medical conditions that they had prior to enlistment which then surfaced or became detrimental to their health as a result of the rigors of boot-camp training.

6.2 General Overview of ELS

Not everyone that is recruited or enlists in the military can become a soldier. The military is a way of life, with its own standards of conduct, unique customs and traditions, and different pressures and expectations. As a new recruit, they must learn to think differently about themselves and others. They face difficult training programs, an abundance of rules and regulations, and lose many of the freedoms enjoyed as a civilian. If the recruit cannot adapt to the military world and demonstrates that they are not succeeding within it, they may be eligible for an entry level performance and conduct discharge. It is available only if they are still in entry level status. ELS is available only if discharge processing is initiated by the command while the recruit is in entry level status, which is the first 180 days of continuous active military service. Military personnel are trained to recognize under-achievers and if they recognize one they will extend effort to improve the performance of the recruit –as noted in the above regulation– rather than risk a request for ELS.

Getting an early discharge is not easy and the procedures can be complicated. Discharge regulations are intended to give commanders control over their troops to maintain good order and discipline. The regulations give commanding officers a great deal of discretion, and only minimal guidelines, for deciding whether or not discharge is appropriate. Policies may differ from one command to another (even within the same base) and a command can change policy without warning. The military normally will not discharge a member with a short-term and treatable condition. A common category of disorders known as "adjustment disorders" are not considered to be of long enough duration to warrant discharge.

The military grants the greatest number of ELS discharges during basic training. Therefore, this discharge is more likely to be granted before basic training is completed, when commanders are less likely to be penalized for "losing" a soldier. After basic training is completed the military has a great deal more invested in the recruit and the new commander is less likely to grant, or even to be familiar with, an entry level performance and conduct discharge.

While an ELS it is not likely to have a negative impact on future employment, some employers may not want to hire someone who could not adapt to the military. Recruits granted ELS are not eligible for veterans' or medical benefits.

6.3 Valid Reasons for ELS

According to Army Regulation 635-200, the following are valid reasons for ELS:

- Inability [to become a soldier]
- Lack of reasonable effort [to become a soldier]
- Failure to adapt to the military environment
- Cannot or will not adapt socially or emotionally to military life and regimen
- Lack of aptitude, ability, motivation or self-discipline.
- Character and behavior not compatible with military service
- Failure to respond to counseling. (11-2, 11-3)

In addition to the above there are several other reasons that are classified as "other designated physical or mental conditions", which are also valid reasons for ELS (AR 635-200, par.5-17):

- Chronic seasickness

- bedwetting or incontinence
- Chronic airsickness
- sleep walking
- severe nightmares
- claustrophobia
- thoughts of suicide
- psychological or emotional distress
- a physical or mental condition that potentially interferes with assignment or performance of duty

A recruit may also be separated for personality disorder, which is defined by the above regulation as "a deeply ingrained maladaptive pattern of behavior of long duration that interferes with the soldier's ability to perform duty." (par. 5-13.a) Any recruit that is seeking separation due to a personality disorder requires psychiatric evaluation.

The following are other reasons for ELS as noted in DOD regulations [which do not directly apply to our situation]:

- parenthood – too much time is taken away from military duty to care for a new-born
- hardship – the recruit becomes sole supporter due to death of a family member
- homosexual activity (immediate discharge)
- disciplinary infractions – wanton and regular negligence resulting in numerous violations of military law. The recruit will be discharged in lieu of court-martial.
- Pregnancy – the female recruit will be transferred to IRR.
- Alcohol or drug abuse with failure at rehabilitation
- Failure to meet body fat standards (obesity)
- Unauthorized absence (AWOL) – although this will often result in court-martial and incarceration in a military prison.

Because all recruits are required to answer negatively as part of the enlistment the questions that pertain to convictions, beliefs or education in conscientious objection to military service and signing Form 3286, which states that the recruit is not a C.O., for this reason it is difficult to acquire ELS due to C.O., however it is possible. In regulation Army Regulation 635-200, which regulates ELS, nowhere is conscientious objection mentioned as a reason for ELS. Only in AR 600-43 is C.O.

mentioned as a valid reason for ELS (par. 3-2), but the procedure is the same whether in entry level status or in active service following completion of boot-camp.

6.4 Approaching the Command

There are 2 methods for seeking an entry level separation:

- The recruit does not request discharge but presents their problems to the command.
- The recruit submits a written request for discharge, including any supporting documentation.

The first step in approaching the command is for the recruit to tell their problems to a chaplain and get a referral to the base counseling center. The recruit must be in the situation that he cannot adapt to military regimen or training: unable to shoot a gun or some other weapon, unable to bayonet a dummy, unable to shout "Kill, kill", unable to march in company carrying a gun or wear a military uniform, and that the vocation of a soldier has become repulsive to the recruit.

The recruit can also request a meeting with the commanding officer to discuss his difficulties. The recruit can approach the command in the role of a patient presenting his problems. By proceeding in this manner the commanding officer may recommend discharge to the command. The recruit must identify problems as specifically as possible. The recruit must provide the military command evidence that he is unable to adapt physically or emotionally to the military and that he cannot be rehabilitated into a performing soldier, and that it is in the best interest of the military to discharge you.

Do not make up problems that do not exist. The recruit may be tempted to mess up on purpose, by deliberately failing tests, performing sluggishly, or even misbehaving. The recruit will not be processed for this separation if the command believes that their problems are manufactured, or that the behavior is consciously undertaken to avoid military service. Any deliberate acts of unsatisfactory performance or misconduct could lead to retention with a loss of future chance of ELS.

When military command determines that a recruit in entry level status is unqualified for further military service by reason of unsatisfactory performance or conduct, and that rehabilitation has failed or will fail the command will initiate separation proceedings. To grant an ELS, the command will view a service member's problems with military duty as unintentional, and issue a notification to the recruit.

The recruit must respond within 7 days using the form in Army Regulation 635-200, Figure 2-4. In our situation the recruit will waive review by an administrative board (item 2), since this does not apply.

The commanding officer will then transmit his recommendation – discharge – to the separation authority – a board of military officials. See Army Regulation 635-200, Figure 2-5 for sample letter. They will review the case, evidence and recommendation and decide. In our situation they will decide in favor of discharge as recommended by the command as in the best interests of the military. (The only time a hearing before an administrative board is required is if the recruit is being discharged for disciplinary reasons, bad conduct, negligence of duties; that is, against the will of the recruit. The administrative hearing is the opportunity for the recruit to defend his retention in the military. This does not apply to our situation.)

Eventually the recruit will be issued DOD Regulation 1332.14, Form 214, Certificate of Release of Discharge from Active Service (See sample copy Appendix XVIII).

6.5 Interval during Proceedings

During the interval between the recruit's initial visit to the command or base counselor regarding his inability to adapt to military regimen and acquisition of a discharge, the recruit is supposed to be separated from regular military training and assigned to some other work on the base. This may or may not occur since it is at the discretion of the command, and retention in military training may be a maneuver to test the sincerity of the recruit. The command may also place the recruit in custody – incarceration – to separate them from the balance of military personnel on the base.

Under no circumstances should the recruit fail to observe any regulations or orders required of them unless they are premeditative attempts by officers for the recruit to return to the military training he is requesting discharge from. In that case the recruit should go to their command and inform them of the situation. Applying for ELS does not excuse the recruit from performing non-training duties, wearing a uniform, or following general orders. Until the recruit is discharged, they are subject to military rules. During processing the recruit may decide that he can no longer cooperate with the military. Non-cooperation, sometimes called resistance, takes many forms. Some recruits refuse to work, obey orders, or wear their uniforms. Others simply go AWOL. Recruits resist for many reasons. Some want to cooperate with the process but find that they can't compromise as much as they had thought. Others become so frustrated with delays in processing that they feel they must resist.

Refusal to follow orders, going AWOL, or refusal to wear a military uniform are all violations of the Uniform Code of Military Justice (UCMJ) and could result in incarceration or even court-martial, and the case for ELS will be closed and the recruit retained in active duty.

6.6 Counseling and Rehabilitation

Prior to the command initiating separation proceedings he must require counseling and rehabilitation of the recruit, as required by DOD 1332.14

> E3.A1.1.7.2. Separation and Rehabilitation. Separation proceedings may not be initiated until the member has been counseled formally concerning deficiencies and has been afforded an opportunity to overcome those deficiencies as reflected in appropriated counseling or personnel records. Counseling and rehabilitation requirements are of particular importance with respect to this reason for separation. Because military service is a calling different from any civilian occupation, a member should not be separated when unsatisfactory performance is the sole reason unless there have been efforts at rehabilitation under standards prescribed by the secretary concerned.

Army regulations also require counseling:

> When a soldier's conduct or performance becomes unacceptable, the commander will ensure that a responsible official formally notified the soldier of his/her deficiencies. At least one formal counseling session is required before separation proceedings may be initiated... In addition, there must be evidence that the soldiers deficiencies continued after the initial formal counseling. Army Regulation 635-200, par. 1-16.b.1.

The extent of counseling is at the discretion of the command. Rehabilitation consists of alternative military training at the base or reassignment to another regiment, and sometimes incarceration. If the command senses that further training on base is useless or detrimental to the new regiment, rehabilitation will be cancelled and ELS proceedings will be initiated.

PART 7

DISCHARGE AS A CONSCIENTIOUS OBJECTOR

7.1 The C.O. and Military Service

Please note **Section 2.1** above for the definition of a C.O. according to the Military Selective Service Act and the Department of Defense.

It is very difficult to acquire a discharge from the military as a C.O. because, as part of the enlistment process, the recruit has verified that he is not opposed to war or military service and that he has not received religious training that would interfere with his ability to perform military service (see **section 2.3** above).

To be released as a C.O., once already enlisted and in active duty, the recruit must prove to military officials the following 3 items specified in DOD 1300.6:

> 5.1.1.1. [he] is conscientiously opposed to participation in war in any form;
> 5.1.1.2. [his] opposition is founded on religious training and belief; and
> 5.1.1.3. [his] position is sincere and deeply held.

The regulations also note the following:

> 5.3.2. Care must be exercised in determining the integrity of belief and the consistency of application. Information presented by the claimant should be sufficient to convince that the claimant's personal history reveals views and actions strong enough to demonstrate that expediency or avoidance of military service is not the basis of his claim.

These definitions are important because the entire claim of the C.O. discharge is based on them. Membership in a church that advocates conscientious objection as a tenet of its creed is not on its own sufficient basis to warrant discharge as a C.O. The recruit must prove C.O. is a deeply held conviction and not a ruse for discharge from the military.

7.2 The C.O. in Active Service

According to Army Regulation 1300.6,

> 4.1.1. Except as provided in Section 4.1.2. of this Directive, no member of the Armed Forces who possessed conscientious objection beliefs before entering military service is eligible for classification as a Conscientious Objector if:
> 4.1.1.1. (1) such beliefs satisfied the requirements for classification as a Conscientious Objector pursuant to Section 6(j) of the Universal Military Training and Service Act, as amended (50 U.S.C. App. 456(j)) and other provisions of law, and (2) he failed to request classification as a Conscientious Objector by the Selective Service System; or
> 4.1.1.2. (1) he requested classification as a Conscientious Objector before entering military service, and (2) such request was denied on the merits by the Selective Service System, and (3) his request for classification as a Conscientious Objector is based upon essentially the same grounds, or supported by essentially the same evidence, as the request which was denied by the Selective Service System.
> 4.1.2. Nothing contained in this Directive renders ineligible for classification as a Conscientious Objector a member of the Armed Forces who possessed Conscientious Objector beliefs before entering military service if (a) such beliefs crystallized after receipt of an induction notice; and (b) he could not request classification as a Conscientious Objector by the Selective Service System because of Selective Service System regulations prohibiting the submission of such requests after receipt of induction notice.

What does this mean?

If a person had convictions of a C.O. prior to the time they voluntarily enlisted into the military and still proceeded to sign AR Form 3286 – or the form pertaining to that branch of the Armed Forces – then that recruit is not eligible for discharge. Only the recruit who did not have beliefs or convictions of conscientious objection against war and military service prior to entering the service, and that such beliefs and convictions were acquired and crystallized after beginning boot-camp training, will be granted the opportunity to request discharge as a C.O. Although a recruit may have had religious instruction in objection to war prior to enlistment and induction, what is important is that this instruction did not create convictions in him of a C.O., or a repulsion to military service and regimen, until after his entrance at boot camp or later during his term of active service. The difficulty for the recruit is in proving such a claim, that these convictions crystallized during military training.

7.3 Process of Application and Discharge

The CCCO recommends that a recruit submit a letter immediately. Write the letter saying, "I have become a conscientious objector to participation in war in any form." Then say that you want to be discharged. Then write, "I understand that until a final decision is made I am to be employed in duties providing minimum conflict with my beliefs." It is also a good idea, if you can, to make a specific request for temporary duty or transfer to an assignment you can accept--for instance, if you're in a combat unit, you can request an assignment that doesn't use weapons, or if none is available, ask for transfer out of your unit to one with noncombatant jobs available.

Submit the letter to the base commanding officer. Keep a copy. This written request may serve one or more purposes.

- It puts the military on notice that you're a C.O..
- It may get you placed on noncombatant duty until the military decides on your case; and
- In some cases, it may get you held in your unit rather than shipped to a combat unit or combat assignment.

The recruit will then be requested to fill out form DA 4187 (Army) (see sample copy Appendix XV), or the form applicable to that branch of the service requesting a reclassification, which is essentially a discharge. In Section III of the form, under Request, the recruit will check the RECLASSIFICATION box and state *to 1-O status,* and check the OTHER box and write *for discharge as a conscientious objector*.

Along with the form answers to 26 questions will be required. There is no form to fill out with the list of questions. They are merely listed in DOD 1300.6, as enclosure 1, and in Army Regulation 600-43, Appendix

B. About 10 to 12 typed pages should constitute a properly submitted answer to the questions. The commanding officer will specify the time frame for submission of completed form DA 4187 and answers to the 26 questions. Any delay on the part of the recruit will be cause for more delay on the part of the military.

The recruit will then be informed that as a result of discharge due to classification as 1-O they will forfeit all benefits due them as a veteran. The recruit will have to sign a statement similar to that of Figure 2-3. This statement will be attached to form DA 4187.

The base commander will schedule an interview of the recruit by a military chaplain and by a psychiatrist (or a medical officer if a psychiatrist is not available). Following these interviews the recruit will face an investigative hearing by a military board.

7.4 During the Interval

Upon receipt of Form DA 4187 the base commander is required to reassign the recruit to duties that provide minimum practical conflict with their asserted beliefs. The extent of this is at the discretion of the base commander. The recruit is still obligated to follow orders assigned them, as stated in DOD 1330.6:

> Unless the Military Service concerned provides otherwise, an applicant shall be required to comply with active duty or transfer orders in effect at the time of his application or subsequently issued and received. During the period applications are being processed, applicants will be expected to conform to the normal requirement of military service and to perform such duties as are assigned. Applicants may be disciplined for violations of the Uniform Code of Military Justice while awaiting action on their applications. (par. 6.9)

Normally this means you'll be put to work as a clerk or warehouse worker or continue to train--except in the study, use, or handling of weapons. You might also be assigned to do nothing, either as a way of harassing you or because there just isn't any suitable assignment for you.

There is some question as to just what duties in the military "conflict as little as possible" with C.O. beliefs. The Department of Defense maintains that "service aboard an armed ship or aircraft or in a combat zone shall not be considered to be combatant duty unless the individual involved is personally and directly involved in the operation of weapons." In the Coast Guard, you can still be ordered to use a handgun.

As mentioned above with recruits awaiting ELS, the military will make life as difficult as possible for the recruit seeking discharge as a C.O. in order to manipulate them into violating some military code. This will then serve as a means for the military to drop all proceedings related to the requested for discharge and either retain the recruit in his regiment or else begin process for court-martial if they refuse. Refusal to follow orders, going AWOL, or refusal to wear a military uniform are all violations of the Uniform Code of Military Justice (UCMJ) and could result in incarceration or even court-martial, and the case for discharge as a C.O. will be closed.

7.5 Questions and Answers

The following are the 26 questions that must be answered by the recruit in his own words and attached to Form DA 4187. An Advisor cannot answer the questions for the recruit because in interviews the recruit will need to defend themselves in their own words. However guides for answering the questions are noted in sub-paragraphs.

1. Full name.

2. Military serial number; and Social Security Account number.

3. Selective Service number.

4. Service address.

5. Permanent home address.

6. Name and address of each school and college attended after age 16 together with the dates of attendance, and the type of school: public, church, military, commercial, etc.

7. A chronological list of all occupations, positions, jobs, or types of work, other than as a student in school or college after age 16 whether for monetary compensation or not. Include the type of work, name of employer, address of employer and the from/to date for each position or job held.

8. All former addresses after age 16 and dates of residence at those addresses.

9. Parent's name and addresses. Indicate whether they are living or deceased.

10. The religious denomination or sect of both parents.

11. Was application made to the Selective Service System (local board) for classification as a Conscientious Objector prior to entry into the Armed Forces? To which local board? What decision was made by the Board, if known?

12. When the applicant has served less than one hundred and eighty (180) days in the Military Service, a statement by him as to whether he is willing to perform work under the Selective Service civilian work program for Conscientious Objectors, if discharged as a Conscientious Objector. Also, a statement of the applicant as to whether he consents to the issuance of an order for such work by his local Selective Service Board.

> In our situation, if the recruit is still in entry level status they will seek a ELS. Otherwise this question does not apply.

13. A description of the nature of the belief which requires the applicant to seek separation from the Military Service or assignment to non-combatant training and duty for reasons of conscience.

> Make it clear that because of your religious or moral training and belief you cannot participate in war. This is more than just wishing to avoid a combat zone. It is a firm decision that it is morally wrong to participate in war in any form. Any association with the military conflicts with your convictions. You should say why you cannot take a noncombatant job in the military. Military officials may easily see why you are

against killing, but may not understand why you aren't willing to serve in some other way.

14. An explanation as to how his beliefs changed or developed, to include an explanation as to what factors (how, when and from whom or from what source training received and belief acquired) caused the change in or development of conscientious objection beliefs.

> Try to show how your present beliefs relate to your earlier training and experiences, both inside and outside the military. You'll want to list the different things that helped you form your beliefs against participating in war and your moral value system in general. Your beliefs about war are part of your overall beliefs.

> Include in your answer experiences you've had since entering the military, which have been important in your decision. Explain how your new experiences in the military make you see that you can't be part of war.

15. An explanation as to when these beliefs became incompatible with military service, and why.

> The military may try to deny your claim if they believe you held C.O. beliefs at the time you enlisted. So it's very important to state clearly that you weren't a C.O. when you enlisted, and what made you change your mind. If you had feelings against war before you entered the military, you are only eligible for discharge or transfer if those feelings matured or crystallized into *objections* after you came face to face with military training and duty. It's the objection to participation that's the important thing. You have to explain what it was that finally made you decide you were against participating in war.

> Also make it clear why you are making the application now and not a month ago or longer. Some people don't think seriously about what they are doing until they get orders for reassignment. The shock of being sent to a combat zone or combat-type training is often what gets someone thinking. If

any of the above applies to you, say so and describe the experiences and your reaction.

16. An explanation as to the circumstances, if any, under which the applicant believes in the use of force, and to what extent, under any foreseeable circumstances.

> This is a trick question to identify police or personal force with war and military aggression. Show the difference between force you accept and force you reject. Why and how the kinds of force you would use are different from war. Keep in mind that you don't have to object to all force or to violence, but only to war. (This question is further discussed below.)

17. An explanation as to how the applicant's daily life style has changed as a result of his beliefs and what future actions he plans to continue to support his beliefs.

> This and the following question concern your sincerity and depth of belief. Since you're in the military and can't change your life style very much, the question may seem unrealistic. But there may be some things you can point to. Do you talk with or write to friends about the problems of conscience and war. Have you talked with other members of the military about conscientious objection? Have you tried to avoid the more warlike aspects of training duty, like rifle range or bayonet training?

> As for the future, you can't be sure how you will act in all situations, but many C.O.s state that they will try to act according to their beliefs--whether or not their requests are approved. Think about what you might like to do when you get your discharge.

18. An explanation as to what in applicant's opinion most conspicuously demonstrates the consistency and depth of his beliefs which gave rise to his claim.

> You are making your application in order to settle the conflict between your conscience and your military duties.

Your application itself may be the strongest, most persuasive evidence that you are trying to act in an honest and consistent manner. The more care and effort that goes into your claim, the more convincing this argument will be.

In addition to actions you've taken on your C.O. claim and any work for peace you've done, be sure to include other actions which show that you try to live by your values. Since you believe in the Bible, state that you read it regularly.

19. Information as to whether applicant has ever been a member of any military organization or establishment before entering upon his present term of service. If so, the name and address of such organization will be given together with reasons why he became a member.

In our situation the response will be "No".

20. A statement as to whether applicant is a member of a religious sect or organization.

Reply as needed.

21. The name of the sect, and the name and location of its governing body or head, if known.

This information on your membership and answers to the subsequent questions through 25 can be acquired from an Advisor or the minister of your congregation.

22. When, where, and how the applicant became a member of said sect or organization.

23. The name and location of any church, congregation or meeting which the applicant customarily attends, and the extent of the applicant's active participation therein.

24. The name, title, and present address of the pastor or leader of such church, congregation or meeting.

25. A description of the creed or official statements, if any, and if they are known to him, of said religious sect or organization in relation to participation in war.

26. A description of applicant's relationships with and activities in all organizations with which he is or has been affiliated, other than military, political, or labor organizations.

In our situation the response would be "None".

Preparing a C.O. application isn't like taking a test. The only right answers are the ones you think are right. You can help yourself to do a good job by using these guidelines:

- Keep your answers as simple as you can. Make them long enough to explain your beliefs, but keep in mind that long answers aren't always better.
- Write what you believe. Don't write about what you don't believe. This saves space, and it's a more positive approach.
- Don't try to convince military officials that they are wrong and you are right. This is just a waste of time. Always say "I" believe that "I" must act in such and such a way.
- Show how your beliefs lead you to object to war and military training.
- Submit a neat application. If you can't type, it's worth the money to have a professional type your claim for you. Every Service requires a typed application.
- Make several copies of your application and keep them in a safe place.

7.6 Letters and References

Letters should definitely be provided by an Advisor, the ministers of your church, and other elders. Try to get at least four letters. Less is all right, and so is a few more. But a few good letters are better than a lot of poor letters.

Letters should be addressed to "The Commanding Officer of (your name)" rather than "To Whom It May Concern" or to you. Typed letters are more likely to be read, but neatly handwritten letters are fine as well.

The writer should explain who he or she is, and how he or she knows you, and should discuss:

- your sincerity;
- the recent change in your beliefs and how they have matured;
- the religious, moral, or ethical basis of your beliefs;

The letters should be sent to you so you can submit all of them at your Investigative Officer hearing. If you and your Advisor think a letter doesn't support you or has wrong information, don't submit it; it is your claim that is at stake. Keep copies of each letter in a safe place.

7.7 Requirement of Interviews

DOD 1300.6 states:

> 6.3. The applicant shall be personally interviewed by a chaplain who shall submit a written opinion as to the nature and basis of the applicant's claim, and as to the applicant's sincerity and depth of conviction. The chaplain's report shall include the reasons for his conclusions. In addition, the applicant will be interviewed by a psychiatrist (or by a medical officer if a psychiatrist is not reasonably available) who shall submit a written report of psychiatric evaluation indicating the presence or absence of any psychiatric disorder which would warrant treatment or disposition through medical channels, or such character or personality disorder as to warrant recommendation for appropriate administrative action. This opinion and report will become part of the "case file." If the applicant refuses to participate or is uncooperative or unresponsive in the course of the interviews, this fact will be included in the statement and report filed by the chaplain and psychiatrist or medical officer.

7.8 Psychiatric Interview

The psychiatrist, psychologist, or medical officer has to decide whether you have any medical disorders which would make you eligible for discharge. You may feel offended by the interview; many C.O.s don't like being suspected of having mental disorders just because they oppose killing and war.

The psychiatrist may comment on your sincerity but doesn't have to. (In the Army and Air Force, the psychiatrist is supposed to make no recommendation for approval or denial of the application.) If you don't cooperate or respond during this interview or the one with the chaplain, the officer is supposed to note it in his or her report. Usually the interview takes only a few minutes, and the psychiatrist's report is brief.

The military psychiatrist could recommend discharge for psychiatric reasons, but be careful not to make the psychiatrist think your C.O. beliefs are a result of emotional problems. And, if you think you might be eligible for discharge on grounds of mental disorder, discuss this interview with your counselor before you do. Some military branches or commands may require you to take a standard personality test before you see the psychiatrist.

7.9 Chaplain's Interview

Don't be surprised if the chaplain is more hostile toward you and your views than any other officer. But there are a number of sympathetic, sensitive chaplains who care a lot about freedom of conscience. In any event, the chaplain is supposed to interview you and "submit a written opinion as to the nature and basis of the applicant's claim, and as to the applicant's sincerity and depth of conviction." He or she must also give the reasons for these conclusions. Again, in the Army and Air Force, the chaplain is supposed to make no recommendation for approval or denial of the application.

Remember that the chaplain's idea of what may be considered religious, ethical, or moral may be narrower than the legal definition discussed earlier in this chapter. If may be wise to visit a 2nd chaplain if the interview with the first turns out to be unsatisfactory, but you'll probably have to set up the 2nd visit on your own.

7.10   Investigative Hearing

The following is stated in DOD 1300.6:

> 6.4.2. The investigating officer will conduct a hearing on the application. The purpose of the hearing is: to afford the applicant an opportunity to present any evidence he desires in support of his application; to enable the investigating officer to ascertain and assemble all relevant facts to create a comprehensive record; and to facilitate an informed recommendation by the investigating officer and an informed decision on the merits by higher authority. In this regard, any failure or refusal of the applicant to submit to questioning under oath or affirmation before the investigating officer may be considered by the officer making his recommendation and evaluation of the applicant's claim. If the applicant fails to appear at the hearing without good cause, the investigating officer may proceed in his absence and the applicant will be deemed to have waived his appearance.

The most important interview is the one with the Investigating Officer. In fact, this "interview" is more of an informal hearing. In the Army, Air Force, and Marines, the IO is appointed by the commander with special court-martial jurisdiction over you (usually the brigade, regiment, or group commander). In the Navy, the appointing authority is your commanding officer; in the Coast Guard it's the district commander. This hearing is extremely important. You should not waive your right to attend it even if the military offers to let you do so. This will probably be the best chance you will get to present your views. If, without a good reason, you don't appear at the interview, it will be assumed that you have waived your rights, and the Investigating Officer will hold the hearing without you and your request will be rejected.

The Investigating Officer's interview has several purposes. It is a chance for you to add evidence or papers to your application before the complete record is forwarded for a final decision. The officer must gather information on your case and then interview you. Finally, the IO is to make an "informed recommendation" on your case so that the higher authority may make an "informed decision." As part of the investigation, the officer may seek out information about you from commanders, supervisors, written records, and other likely sources of important information.

You may present whatever evidence you wish, give any sworn or unsworn statements you think may help your case, and have witnesses to give sworn statements. This is the time to add to the file any reference letters, church statements on conscientious objection, or other papers that you haven't already attached to your application. It is also a chance for you to look at and comment on everything in the file, including the opinion of the chaplain and the psychiatrist and any other evidence gathered by the Investigating Officer, if you haven't already done so. The hearing is informal, except that all oral testimony is given under oath or affirmation.

If your religious beliefs require you to affirm rather than swear, you have the right to "affirm" that your testimony is true.

You have the right to have witnesses testify in your support at the hearing. If you can think of people who could offer evidence of your sincerity, ask to have them testify. People who wrote supporting letters for your claim are especially important witnesses. By attending the hearing, such witnesses give additional weight to their testimony of your sincerity.

While the military won't pay for the personal or travel expenses of your witnesses, local commanders are supposed to "render all reasonable assistance in making available military members of his command requested by the applicant as witnesses." If you want fellow service members or officers to serve as witnesses, you should, as soon as possible, request in writing that the local command make those persons available. If your commander does not help, and if those witnesses do not appear at the hearing, you should explain in your application why you wanted them to come, attach a copy of the letter to the commander, and state that they did not appear at the hearing. All witnesses should be notified as soon as possible of the hearing date, time, and place. In addition, you will be allowed to question any other witnesses the Investigating Officer calls or who volunteer to come.

Just prior to and on the day of the hearing you should meet with your Advisor and any of your witnesses to prepare for the hearing. It can be particularly helpful to role play questions with your counselor to help you prepare for the hearing. You can request that your witnesses be present during the interview. If this is allowed, it could give you additional support and be especially helpful to any witness who is also a C.O. applicant.

Bring a copy of your application and any additional material, as well as a list of those who will testify and those not available for testimony. After taking the oath or affirmation, you or your Advisor can review all items in the investigating officer's file and submit any new information.

Usually the Investigating Officer will have some questions to ask. Some of these are likely to be routine. Others may be very difficult or hostile. If you don't have an answer to a question, say so and then explain why. You don't have to know the answer to every problem in order to be a conscientious objector. And if you say honestly that you find a question difficult, your sincerity and truthfulness may be to your benefit. Do make clear throughout the interview that you know you're against all war and can't be part of it.

Either before or after the questioning, you should call your witnesses, one by one. They must also take the oath or affirmation before they testify. All should state their relationship with you and why they offered to testify.

If the Investigating Officer has summoned any other witnesses, you or your Advisor can question them if necessary. The possible questions that may be asked are codified in Appendix I, along with a suggested answer, however the answer must always be the conviction of the C.O.

7.12   After the Hearing

The military base then has 90 days to submit the forms and all documents to Headquarters, and this can be extended to 180 days at their discretion. The recruit should expect the process to take about a year.

The percentage of claims approved varies from Service to Service and from year to year. In the 12 years prior to the Persian Gulf War (1991), more than 80% of C.O. claims were approved.

Once your immediate commander has been notified, you should be out within 10 days. The discharge will be Honorable, unless you had refused to obey orders or refused to wear the uniform while your claim was pending; then you may get a General Discharge (Under Honorable Conditions). The discharge will be for the "Convenience of the Government," but your separation papers will give "conscientious objection" as the reason for discharge.

7.13   Negative Decision

If your application is turned down, you're in a tough position. The next step as a C.O. is court martial and imprisonment, since you will continue to refuse military service. The last alternative would be flight or migration, but then you would be a fugitive from military justice, and in the long run, matters may be worse for you. Previous history is that imprisonment is normally from 1 to 3 years with a dishonorable discharge.

PART 8

EXEMPTION FROM CONSCRIPTION AS A CONSCIENTIOUS OBJECTOR

8.1 The C.O. and Military Service

The Selective Service System (Draft Board) has a due process for individuals to acquire a conscientious objector classification and not be required to perform military service. **US Code title 50, appendix 456 (j) of the Military Selective Service Act** provides exemption for conscientious objectors.

> Nothing contained in this title shall be construed to require any person to be subject to combatant training and service in the Armed Forces of the United States who, by reason of religious training and belief, is conscientiously opposed to participation in war in any form.

The C.O. applicant will follow due process to acquire classification as a CO, as permitted them by the above section of law. If it is denied him, then he will proceed using legitimate means to avoid conscription, and endure whatever should occur. As with all correspondence with the government, make a copy and an extra of all correspondence and documents that you forward to or receive from the government.

8.2 The Selective Service and the Historic Peace Church

The policy of the Selective Service System towards those denominations earlier recognized as official peace churches changed about 1980. From Viet-Nam War the Selective Service acquired information regarding the religious affiliation of conscientious objectors: many members of historic militant churches, such as Catholic, Lutheran, Episcopalian, Methodist, had registered as C.O., and acquired an exemption to military service; and at the same time members of historic peace churches, such as Quaker, Mennonite, Friends, and Molokans, had been conscripted into the military with no objection and served their term of enlistment.

The attitude of the Federal Government toward religions is specified in the First Amendment to the Constitution, **"Congress shall make no law respecting an establishment of religion..."** For the Selective Service to acknowledge one denomination as an official historic peace church and allow its members precedence to acquire a C.O. exemption, while not allowing this same treatment toward another denomination was now understood as favoring one denomination over another, and therefore unconstitutional.

Beginning in 1980, the Selective Service began to treat all denominations equally. At the present and should there occur conscription in the future, every member of every denomination will be treated equally in regards to their request for a C.O. exemption, with no denomination to be favored over another.

The latest edition of the Selective Service regulations (32 CFR Ch. VVI), July of 2001, states the following in paragraph 1636.7, **"Boards may not give preferential treatment to one religion over another, and all beliefs whether of a religious, ethical, or moral nature are to be given equal consideration."**

Under the latest edition of the SSS regulations, the members of all denominations and religions and convictions who are seeking to be C.O.s will be treated equally and without preference.

8.3 The Lottery and Induction Notices

If and when the Congress and the President reinstate a military draft, the Selective Service System would conduct a National Draft Lottery to determine the order in which young men would be drafted. The first priority group that will be called will be those who turn twenty in the current calendar year. In 2008, if a draft began, the first priority group would be those born in 1988. In the unlikely case that the entire first priority group is exhausted, the next older age group will be called. The sequence goes through age group 25, takes a group with extended liability through age 34, then calls those 19, and ends with those 18 and a half. It is very unlikely, however, that more than one or two age groups would be reached.

More than half the draftees are expected to fail the physical or mental standards, and still others will obtain postponements, deferments, exemptions, or conscientious objector classification. Therefore, more than twice as many as are needed will have to be ordered to appear for examination and induction.

There are 2 manners of induction that are available to be utilized by the SSS. The first is the RIPS (Registrant Integrated Processing System) which is the peace time or non-emergency draft, a means of keeping the ranks of the military full if volunteer enlistment is below the personnel requirements of the armed forces. The second is the RIMS (Registrant Information and Management System), which is utilized during active war time to call to service conscripts according to the demand of the war. Both manners of induction will be discussed, and the method for the C.O. to acquire an exemption from military service. With either method, the SSS will send notices to men as their number appears in the lottery. The C.O. must remember that time is of the essence whenever he receives any correspondence from the SSS, because a delayed response may void his claim.

The medical examinations are performed at the MEPS (Military Entrance Processing Station).

Exemptions at the present are few compared to those during WW2 and Vietnam. If a person is enrolled full time in an educational institution, then he is deferred only to the end of the semester. Being married does not matter anymore, and being a sole survivor will only place you in some area perhaps not in direct combat. Hardship is very difficult to prove, and the only valid exemption for many is to become a minister or be a ministerial student, yet this will be hard to prove to the Draft Board.

8.4 RIPS: Non-Emergency Conscription

8.4.1   The SSS will send a notice of examination and induction, SSS Form 233 (Appendix IX) to the draftee, along with a copy of SSS Form 233P (Appendix X). The draftee is ordered to appear for an examination: mental, physical and intellectual. If the draftee fails the examination, he will be classified 4F, unfit for military service. If the draftee passes the examination, he will be classified 1A, available for military service. The draftee will be sent a letter from the SSS indicating that he is eligible for induction when the SSS deems another soldier is needed by the military. Along with the letter will be SSS Form 8 (Appendix II), which will allow the draftee to select an exemption from the list when he is ordered for induction. SSS regulations 1633.2(a) state that a claim cannot be made until the registrant has received an order for induction.

8.4.2 The C.O. will follow the directions on Form 233 and go to the MEPS whose address is noted in the form and have the examination performed within the time frame noted, because, as noted above, half the draftees will fail the examination, and you may also fail. If the C.O. fails to appear for examination, or if the C.O. returns Form 233P (Appendix X) with the waiver signed, then the C.O. is waving and forfeiting his right to medical disqualification if his C.O. claim is granted. This means that the C.O. will have to work 2 years alternative service, even though he may have some disqualifying condition. If the C.O. claim is not granted by the Draft Board, then the draftee cannot apply for any other exemption and he will be immediately conscripted into the military when he receives an induction notice.

8.4.3 If the C.O. passes the medical examination, then he will wait for an induction notice, SSS Form 262, from the SSS should the military require him. If the military does not require him, then all is well.

8.4.4 If the C.O. who passes the medical examination needs to be inducted, then he will receive SSS Form 262 (Appendix XIII). At this point, time is of the essence. The C.O. must immediately fill out SSS Form 8, and check the line next to CONSCIENTIOUS OBJECTOR, and any others that you feel that you can qualify for. (Do not check any boxes that you will not qualify for, since this will make it more difficult for you in the future.) The line C.O. Discharge refers to those already completing Alternative Service. The local Draft Board office must receive a completed and signed SSS Form 8 before the ordered date of induction. The C.O. will then *not* appear for induction, but wait for a response from the local Draft Board.

8.4.5   Upon receipt of SSS Form 8, the Draft Board will forward SSS Form 22 (Appendix III and IV) to the C.O. The form must be filled out and documents attached and returned to the Draft Board before the date noted at the top of the form. In Part I, the C.O. will check Box 2: exemption from all training and service in the armed forces (Class 1-O). The C.O. will write a response to the questions in Part II (see Section 8.6 for the manner of answering the questions), and list all the documents that you are submitting with Form 22. The C.O. will sign and date the Form and return it.

8.4.6   Time is of the essence with Form 22. Normally the time frame to complete all the items are under 10 calendar days. You must get letters from ministers and people you know who will testify to your convictions and will attest to the sincerity of your claim as a C.O. and include these letters with the Form. See Section 8.8 for more information. As with all correspondence, keep a copy for yourself. You are responsible that letters of support are filed with your claim.

8.4.7   After the Draft Board reviews SSS Form 22 and the attached documents, they will send you a letter requesting your presence at a Board Hearing. Section 8.7 describes the criteria that must be satisfied at the Hearing to prove your sincerity and convictions as a C.O. Also Appendix I has a list of questions that may be presented to you, along with suggested responses. If the C.O. does not appear for his Hearing, and does not provide a written explanation for the reason of his failure to appear and a request for another hearing, then the Draft Board will deny the claim.

8.4.8   If the Draft Board grants the C.O. his claim, then he will receive a notice classifying him 1-O, SSS Form 110 (Appendix VI). The SSS will issue an order for him to perform alternative service, either SSS Form 152 (Appendix 152) or SSS Form 155 (Appendix VIII). See Section 8.10 regarding Alternative Service.

8.4.9   The same Form 110 will also indicate if his request for 1-O was denied and what his new classification is. If this is the case, then the C.O. must begin the appeal process (see section 8.9 below).

8.5   **RIMS: Wartime Conscription**

8.5.1   During wartime, the SSS is required to have conscripts ready for induction within 10 days from the date the induction order is written. This means that the draftee has just a few days to respond to his induction notice.

8.5.2   The SSS will send a notice of induction, SSS Form 252 (Appendix XI and XII) to the draftee. He is ordered to appear at the MEPS for a medical examination at the place and time specified on the induction notice. If the draftee fails the examination, he will be classified 4F, unfit for military service. If the draftee passes the examination, he will be classified 1A, available for military service and will be immediately inducted into the military.

8.5.3   When receiving the induction notice Form 252, the C.O. must immediately write a letter to the Draft Board, informing them that he wants to file a claim for reclassification as a conscientious objector. This is stated on Form 9 back page, the paragraph at the bottom (Appendix XII). SSS regulations 1633.2(a) state that a claim cannot be made until the registrant has received an order for induction. Time again is of the essence in this situation and the draftee needs to write his own letter and have it delivered to the Draft Board. When a request for reclassification is filed by the day before you are to appear at the MEPS, you should not appear. You should await the Forms from SSS to document your claims. Your induction is delayed until your classification can be determined.

8.5.4   If you receive a copy of SSS Form 252A, Order to Report for Induction Second Notice, then the Draft Board probably did not receive your letter requesting reclassification. Now you need to send another letter or better to deliver the letter yourself to the Draft Board and request a receipt for the letter.

8.5.5   Once the Draft Board receives and reviews your request for reclassification, you will receive SSS Form 22. Again you only have less than 10 days to complete the form and answer the questions and acquire letters of support, just as in Sections 8.4.5 and 8.4.6 above.

8.5.6   As with the RIPS procedure, the Board Hearing will follow and a determination regarding classification as a C.O. See Section 8.4.7, 8 and 9 above.

8.6 Selective Service Form 22 Questions and Answers

The worksheet that follows list the questions from Form 22, the Selective Service System documentation form for COs facing the draft, and explains the manner of answering them. Every person filing for a C.O. exemption must fill out this form with his answers to these questions.

QUESTION 1: **Describe your beliefs which are the reasons for your claiming conscientious objection to combatant military training and service or to all military training and service.**

This question asks you to describe in some detail and as honestly as possible, the basic principles by which you guide your life. You should describe those values which are of utmost importance to you, such as God, Bible study, love, truth, etc., and why these beliefs are in conflict with participation in war or military service. Quoting from the Gospels or other religious texts will formulate your own statement of conscientious opposition to war. You should begin by saying that you are conscientiously opposed to war, and then describe the beliefs that lead you to such opposition. Also state that you cannot be a non-combatant, because you would still be in the military.

QUESTION 2: **Describe how and when you acquired these beliefs.**

In answering this question, you should include anything of significance which helped you to form your beliefs. Mention any religious training you have had, including your attendance of church, Sunday school, Bible classes. The influence of clergy, teachers, family members, books, membership in organizations and experiences in your life should be listed. Be specific. You need to show that strong influences in your life have stimulated you to think clearly and seriously about not participating in war.

You must also include when you formed your conviction of conscientious objection to military service and training. The Selective Service calls this "crystallization," referring to that point in your life when you came to the conclusion that war and military service was wrong, and this became a specific and personal religious conviction of yours.

QUESTION 3: **Explain what most clearly shows that your beliefs are deeply held. You may wish to include a description of how your beliefs affect the way you live.**

Select the best illustrations of your convictions. List your present activities in the church. You can discuss how your future plans are strongly affected by a commitment to those beliefs. Describe kind of employment you have or plan to have which reflect your commitment. Discuss any public expression, written or oral, you have given to your beliefs. Describe your lifestyle, mention your life's goals as you have set them, and show how they are an outgrowth of your beliefs. This question allows you to demonstrate the sincerity with which you hold your beliefs.

8.7   The Draft Board Hearing

According to the latest rules of the Selective Service, a C.O. can have 4 people with him during his Draft Board hearing. Three of them would be character references while 1 would be an Advisor. There are basically 3 criteria that the C.O. must prove to the Draft Board that he is a genuine CO, and not a draft dodger. These criteria define a C.O. in the Selective Service Regulations:

1.   Is he opposed to war in any form?

A C.O. does not need to be opposed to all forms of violence, but only to the violence and aggression that occurs as a result of war. The C.O. must be against *all* war, that he refuses to bear arms or participate in *any* war, not just against a particular war or against a particular military conflict, like a revolt or revolution. The response of the Draft Board will be examples, like the Revolutionary War or World War 2 against Germany and Japan, or the Iraqi terrorist war. The genuine C.O. will not participate in any war, regardless of the cause or reason of the war.

2.   Does his objection arise from a firm conviction?

A C.O. objects to war because of religious training and belief. Reasons that are political, humanitarian, sociological, economic, or just personal, are not acceptable. The C.O. must testify that he possesses moral, ethical or religious convictions that he considers central in his life, and that arise as a result of belief in a supreme being that has authority over his life that transcends the authority of the state. The reason cannot be a simple personal code, but must be a person's firmly held conviction that will not permit him to be part of war or military training under any circumstances. (The Selective Service will also permit a C.O. who is an atheist to acquire an exemption if he can prove that his convictions have the same affect on his life as would those that are dictated by a supreme being.)

New Testament teachings, of course, will prove this point.

3. Is the objector sincere?

This is the most difficult part of the hearing. The C.O. must demonstrate to the board by way of his life and conduct that he is sincere: you attend church regular, are involved in activities that promote the society, you have an honest job or vocation, you have a clean record. This is where the 3 people with you are to your favor. They should be able to testify to your sincerity by providing additional witness: high morality, good conduct, honesty, and tell the members of the Draft Board that you are sincere.

8.8   Letters of Support for Conscientious Objector Claims

Letters of support for a claim to be classified as a conscientious objector are vital. Good letters of support could be a deciding factor when a C.O. claim is considered. It would be much more difficult for a draft board to maintain that a person is insincere if there are several supporting letters from respected individuals stating otherwise. The writers of these letters may be people you choose later to be witnesses at the hearing of your claim before the draft board.

Choose references carefully. Try to get a good cross-section of people who know you -- teachers, relatives, classmates, friends. Any statements your references can make verifying the sincerity or strength of your beliefs would be significant. They can help you most by answering in their letters the following questions:

1) What is your relationship with the applicant, and how long have you known him/her?

2) Do you believe that the applicant is sincere in his/her claim as a conscientious objector?

3) To the best of your knowledge, has the applicant's conduct since arriving at this belief been consistent with the claim being made?

4) Do you believe the applicant's claim is based on deeply-held moral, ethical or religious beliefs, however broadly defined? If possible, give examples of influences or training in the life of the applicant which you think might have led to the development of his or her beliefs.

These letters should be approximately one page in length, typed or clearly written, and addressed, "To Whom it May Concern." The person writing a letter of support should include your name, address, and Selective Service number. If you receive a letter that is vague, inaccurate or doesn't speak to the four points listed earlier, do not include it in your file. It might prove detrimental.

8.9   The District and the National Appeal Boards

The appeal process begins when a C.O. is dissatisfied with his Local Board's decision about his reclassification request and initiates an appeal, and usually due to his classification as 1-A, fit for military service. If the C.O. is denied his request for a 1-O classification, he will receive a Notice of Classification, SSS Form 110 (Appendix VI) and the action of the Local Board will be noted. The first line of appeal is to the District Appeal Board. To file an appeal, the C.O. must check the 2 boxes at the bottom of Form 110 and sign and date, and send the letter to the Local Board within 15 days from the date that is on Form 110. Include with the Form 110, a letter describing why you feel the decision of the Local Board was incorrect and attach correspondence and documents that you feel will assist the District Board with a decision in your favor.

The District Appeal Board will review the file and will send the C.O. a letter requesting his presence at a review. The C.O. must provide his own travel and expenses to wherever the place the Appeal Board selects for the personal appearance. In this situation, the C.O. is only allowed an advisor to accompany him. The meeting will be a similar interview to that of the Local Board. (If the C.O. fails to appear without good reason, the District Board will make a determination on its own, and will uphold the decision of the Local Board.) After the meeting, the Appeal Board will make its decision and forward it to the CO.

If the C.O. receives a 1-O classification, he will proceed with Alternative Service. If not, then the next step is an Appeal to the President, which is actually an appeal to the National Appeal Board. There are no forms supplied by the SSS for this purpose, and the C.O. must write a personal letter of request for a Presidential Appeal. The letter should describe why you feel the decision of the District Board was incorrect and attach correspondence and documents that you feel will assist the National Board with a decision in your favor.

The National Appeal Board will review the file and send the C.O. a letter requesting his presence at a review. The C.O. must provide his own travel and expenses to wherever the place the National Board selects for the personal appearance. In this situation, the C.O. is only allowed an advisor to accompany him. The meeting will be a similar interview to that of the Local and District Boards. (If the C.O. fails to appear without good reason, the National Board will make a determination on its own, and will uphold the decision of the District Board.) After the meeting, the Appeal Board will make its decision and forward it to the CO.

If the C.O. receives a 1-O classification, he will proceed with Alternative Service. If not, then the C.O. will be reclassified according to the decision of the National Appeal Board, and they usually uphold the decision of the District Board. If this is a 1-A classification, then the C.O. is in a dilemma, because this is where the appeals process ends. Failure to report for induction will lead to arrest and trial for violation of Selective Service regulations and this may result in imprisonment up to 5 years and up to $250,000 fine. Past history has indicated that the sentence is between 1 and 3 years and the fine is usually waved. The C.O. will refuse induction and accept the sentence of the court.

8.10   Alternative Service

Conscientious Objectors classified 1-O will be assigned to civilian work in the national health, safety or interest. You may present your own choice of qualifying jobs for approval, otherwise, you will be assigned by the Alternative Service Office Manager to a job selected by a computer match of employer needs and alternative service worker skills. The C.O. will receive a copy of SSS Form 162 (See Appendix XIV), Job Placement Order, from the Draft Board, which will assign a job to the C.O., if he has not found a job on his own. You can appeal to a Civilian Review Board a job assignment which conflicts with your conscience.

Alternative Service of 24 continuous months in some government approved employment is required of all conscientious objections. During World War 2, this was in Civilian Public Service camps. During Korean War and Viet-Nam War the alternative service was at some charity organization or hospital. The employer has the advantage in this situation, as they know that the C.O. is in a bind and needs to work 24 months of continuous alternative service to satisfy the requirements of the SSS. Often this work is minimum wage or low pay and without a future, so the employment becomes tedious or monotonous.

Failure to complete 24 months of continuous service can result in any one of the following penalties:

I.   Five (5) years imprisonment
II. Fine up to $25,000.
III. Both I and II combined.
IV. Induction into the military
V.   The requirement to again perform 24 months of alternative service, with no credit for the amount completed.

This decision will be made by the Draft Board after another hearing or if the C.O. refuses to cooperate with the Draft Board. Past history indicates that the Draft Board will not be lenient to a person who abandons Alternative Service.

APPENDIX I:

Possible Questions asked at Interviews and Hearings

You will be asked many questions during your required interviews. Your interviewers may be friendly or hostile, straightforward or subtle. You must be cautious or else they will lead you into a trap. Make your answers direct and sincere. You don't have to convince your interviewers that you are right, only that you really believe what you say you believe. If you don't have a good answer in your own mind, it's all right to say that you haven't arrived at an answer for a particular question. Nobody knows all the answers.

Often C.O.s are asked what they would substitute for military force as a method of defense. You don't have to have a complete plan for nonviolent defense – or any plan at all – in order to qualify as a C.O. But for many C.O.s nonviolent resistance is one way of defending one's country and one's principles all at once. And many believe that peace can never come about through violent means, but only through nonviolent ones. Keep in mind that, in order to gain C.O. status, you don't have to present a complete philosophy of nonviolence, but that you will not be participant of any war in any form.

Personal self-defense is not war. What must be proven is that you are now against all war in any form, that you are sincere in your convictions and that you can prove this sincerity with your new life and new attitude.

The questions below are real and have been asked, along with thousands of others. You won't be asked all of them, and you may be asked none of them, but the various interviews will include questions similar to these. Recommendations for an answer are noted in sub-paragraphs.

- Do you doubt that God exists?
     I have no doubt that God exists.

- Is your conscientious objection to war deeply rooted in your own free-thinking and personal opinions?
     Yes.

- How can you say that your belief is religious?
  > It is based on the New Testament teaching of Jesus Christ.

- Is your objection to killing or being killed?
  > Killing. I do not fear being killed for the sake of the Gospel.

- What does your church say about war?
  > This is a matter of personal religious conviction and not necessarily that of the denomination I am a member of.

- Why do most members of your church support military force?
  > This is not the case – or yes, this is the case (depends on your situation)

- Where in the Bible do you find anything which forbids you to defend your country?
  > Jesus said, "Do not resist evil," (Matt 5:39) which we interpret as force or military aggression against ourselves.

- Why did Christ say, "He that hath no sword, let him buy one"?
  > This pertains to those Jews who would not accept his Gospel of peace and would fight against the Romans during the war of 66-70 AD.

- Why did Christ say, "Render unto Cæsar that which is Cæsar's"?
  > We pay taxes, as specified in Rom 13:7.

- Why did Christ say, "I came not to bring peace, but a sword"?
  > This is figurative. The sword represents the separation in families: some would accept Jesus as Messiah, while others would not.

- What would you do if God told you to defend your country?
  > I would become involved in evangelical work, because the defense is against sin and its consequences and its bad effects on society.

- How do you explain all the wars in the Old Testament?
    > This was a concession by God due to the barbaric nature of early civilizations; it was not his perfect will. The perfect will of God materialized in the gospel of peace taught by Jesus.

- Do you think America's millions who killed and died in wars were immoral to kill?
    > War cannot be justified. And I am very sorry that this occurred in the past.

- How about the Christian doctrine of approval for just wars?
    > I do not recognize any doctrine for approval of any wars.

- Is it ever an honor to die for your country if you die keeping the enemy from conquering it?
    > No.

- Do you think that combat soldiers who believe they serve God in serving their country are misled?
    > Every person conducts himself the manner he feels is right. Every person must follow and deal with his own conscience and convictions.

- Can no war be just and necessary regardless of the situation?
    > There is no justification to war or military aggression.

- Do you believe in Romans 13:1-8 of the New Testament, in which it states that God ordains the governing authorities to be servants of God for the good of the governed?
    > This pertains to the internal police force. The police provide internal security. They cannon be compared or equated with the armed forces whose purpose is war.

- Is there any possibility at all that your C.O. application comes out of a feeling of uncertainty, insecurity, or fear of military hardships?
    > No. Because I am willing to face the hardship that may occur as a result of my convictions as a C.O.

- Why are there no atheists in foxholes?

    Everyone believes in God in times of distress because they realize there is no help from a human.

- Does God love that dying American infantry soldier on the battlefield?

    I am sure He does.

- Would he want someone like you to try to save his life?

    I would be willing to provide the love of Christ to soldiers for them to follow the same path I am on so he would not have to face death on a battlefield.

- Does "loving one's neighbor as oneself" ever include being a medic?

    Yes. But the definition of neighbor is the person who has a sincere concern for my welfare according to the parable of Jesus.

- Would it be a high honor for you to die for our country if you did so while helping to save the life of a dying American soldier?

    I would accomplish more if I were to die while employed in a life-long effort in areas that promote the moral advancement of the country.

- Can you say that a medic helping a dying soldier is an immoral act and can never be an expression of God's love?

    For the person helping another on the battlefield, it is the manner that he chooses to express God's love. For myself I would prefer to show God's love in areas off the battlefield.

- If you don't believe in killing, why let a wounded soldier die?

    I am willing to testify to my faith by leading others on the path of being a C.O. so they do not find themselves dying on the battlefield.

- Do you respect and follow the religion of your parents?

    Yes or, No, depending on your situation, and explain.

- Did you arrive at your decision to apply for C.O. by your own personal ideas alone?

  > Yes; or, No, I did have discussion with others on this topic.

- Did books you read have most to do with influencing your request for C.O. status?

  > Reading the New Testament (or some other religious text).

- Since you say you have been a C.O. for only 2 months, might your conscience not change back again 2 months from now?

  > I have acquired a repulsion to military service since joining, which will remain with me for the balance of my life.

- Who helped you prepare your C.O. application?

  > A member of my congregation.

- Are these really your own beliefs?

  > Yes.

- Do you honestly think the Armed Forces should be abolished?

  > Yes. God will protect us and install peace if we as a nation place on faith in Him and live according to the gospel. Even if there is an attack or invasion, non-resistance will reduce the damage and devastation than retaliation or defense.

- What method would you use to resist evil?

  > God permits the use of an internal police force.

- Would you forcibly restrain individual law breakers?

  > According to Rom 13, God permits the state to install a police force for internal security.

- Would you use force to preserve anything you believe in?

  > Anything is a difficult question. I would do my best not to utilize force but only the situation will tell.

- Would you use force to prevent a maniac from killing an innocent person? From killing you? From killing himself?

  I would do my best to reduce the violence or damage to occur.

- Wasn't Hitler a maniac?

  From what I heard he was. But adding further aggression to overthrown someone you feel to be a dictator interferes with the words of God, "Vengeance is mine. I will repay."

- Can't non-destructive force, such as strikes and boycotts, be just as painful and destructive as physical violence?

  I will not either participate in strikes or boycotts; but these still cannot be equated with organized warfare.

- If someone were attacking your mother, would you try to stop him or would you call the police?

  I would do the best I could to minimize injury, and yes, I would call the police. It is their responsibility to provide security.

- Didn't Jesus use violence in driving the money-changers from the temple?

  Yes. But it was His Father's house; but this cannot be equated with organized warfare.

- Do you think the federal government was right in using military force as it has in riots, disorders, and racial strife?

  The police have the responsibility to provide internal security for the country.

- Do you believe in the kind of force the police often have to use to stop killer criminals from murdering others?

  The apostle in Romans 13 allows the police to use capital punishment as a means of securing internal security for the residents of the state. But this cannot be equated with military aggression or war.

- Are you trying to influence others to become conscientious objectors?

    I pray to God that others will also be enlightened as I have and will follow the same path. Hopefully I will serve as an example for them.

- How can you *prove* you're a C.O.?

    The fact that I have applied for reclassification, proceeded in the manner I have requesting discharge, and now testify to you, is my proof.

- What will you do if your application is denied?

    Re-apply.

- Why do you take your place in a society organized by force and then refuse to fight its wars?

    There have always been C.O.s in America since the initial Europeans settled here, and they arrived here for reasons of religious liberty, which reason also applies to myself.

- Why do you pay taxes?

    To support the civil government, as the apostle said to do in Romans 13:7.

- If you really believe these things, why can't you just write a book or speak out about your beliefs after you finish your enlistment?

    I may plan to do what you recommend, but I cannot further my military career because my conscience no longer allows me to do so.

- Wouldn't people have more respect for what you have to say knowing that you served your country?

    Some would. Some would not. It depends on whether the person I speak with has the same convictions as myself or not.

- Aren't you bringing a great deal of dishonor on your family?

    No. My family supports my decision. Or, I must trust my convictions.

- Do you think the authority of your conscience is much more reliable than the consciences of most Americans?

  I do not know what the conscience is of most Americans. Every person must follow their own.

- Do you realize that you are helping to destroy this society?

  Quite the opposite. I am working to benefit the society by reducing its aggression and expenditures in manufacture of military equipment and weapons, and to save lives that would otherwise perish on the battlefield.

- Wasn't the Revolutionary War fought so you can have religious freedom?

  No, the reason was taxation without representation. Religious freedom predates political freedom. The original settlers arrived in America seeking religious freedom. Many of these initial settlers were pacifists.

- What about capital punishment for capital crimes?

  I am likewise opposed to capital punishment.

The recruit must realize that the information related is public, recorded and will determine the recruits sincerity and depth of belief. Prior to the interviews and hearing the recruit should study all of the questions and together with an Advisor compile mental answers to them all.

Local Board/Area Office
Street Address
City, State, ZIP

SELECTIVE SERVICE SYSTEM
CLAIM FOR RECLASSIFICATION
(RIPS)

Date of Issuance

Registrant's Name and SSN   Social Security Number
Street Address   Random Sequence Number
City, State, Zip   Processing Number

Do we have your correct address? If not, cross out the incorrect information above and write in the correct information.

❑   If you made corrections to your address above, and if you wish to have your
claim considered by the office nearest this new address. place a check in box.

PART I: CLAIM FOR RECLASSIFICATION

All claims for reclassification must be made at the same time. Check each statement below which applies to you, sign
and date the form, and return it to the Area Office shown above within ten days from the date of issuance.

_____ Conscientious objector	_____ State or federal elected public
_____ CO discharge	official or judge of court of record
_____ Hardship to dependents	_____ Active military or uniformed service
_____ Hardship discharge	_____ Prior military or uniformed service
_____ Ministerial student	_____ Reserve or National Guard member
_____ Minister of religion	(including ROTC)
_____ Alien or dual national	_____ Surviving son or brother

Do not send any supporting documents with this form to prove your claim. Your Area Office will contact you if any
documents are needed and will provide instructions on where and when they should be forwarded.

PART II: STUDENT STATUS

❑   If you are not making a claim for reclassification, but are attending high school
or college full time, place a check in box.

PART III: CERTIFICATION

I certify that the information I have provided on this form is true, accurate and complete to the best of my knowledge
and belief.

_____   _____
(Registrant's Signature)   (Date)

SSS FORM 8 (AUG 2000)

11-2

APPENDIX II: SSS FORM 8

71

SELECTIVE SERVICE SYSTEM

Registrant Claim Form
(RIMS)

FOR SSS USE ONLY

AOTB SUMMARY

CON	ENTERED BY	DATE ENTERED

1. PRINT YOUR FULL LEGAL NAME

Last   First   Middle   Jr., Sr., II, etc.

2. CURRENT MAILING ADDRESS

Number and street or RFD   Apt. No.

City   State   Zip Code

3. Is the address in item 2 above the same as the address on your induction order? Yes ☐   No ☐

If you checked "no" and wish to have your claim considered by the office nearest this new address, check here. ☐

4. Local Board No. _____
state _____
(see page 1 of induction order)

5. Selective Service Number

6. Date of Birth (Month, Day, Year)

7. Daytime telephone number
(Include area code)

READ THE INSTRUCTIONS FOR COMPLETION ON THE REVERSE OF THIS FORM.

Complete this form only after you have received your Order to Report for Induction. All claims for postponement of induction, and all claims for reclassification, must be made at the same time. Make all claims on this same form, and submit it to your Area Office listed on your induction order, before the date you are scheduled to report for induction.

DO NOT send any supporting documents with this form to prove your claim. Your Area Office will inform you if any documents are needed and will provide instructions on where and when they should be forwarded.

8. CLAIM FOR POSTPONEMENT OF INDUCTION

☐ College Student (Full Time)
☐ High School Student (Full Time)
☐ ROTC Applicant
☐ Cadet/Midshipman (Accepted Applicant in Next Scheduled Class)
☐ Religious Holiday Observance
   Name of Holiday: _____
   Date Holiday Begins: _____
   Date Holiday Ends: _____
☐ Scheduled for State or National Board Licensing/Certification Examination
☐ Temporary Disabling Illness/Injury (Self)
☐ Emergency Condition(s) in Immediate Family

9. CLAIM FOR RECLASSIFICATION

☐ Conscientious Objector
☐ CO Discharge
☐ Hardship to Dependents
☐ Hardship Discharge
☐ Ministerial Student
☐ Minister of Religion
☐ Alien or Dual National
☐ State or Federal Elected Public Official Or Judge of Court of Record
☐ Active Military or Uniformed Service
☐ Prior Military or Uniformed Service
☐ Reserve or National Guard Member
☐ Disabling Physical/Mental Condition
☐ Surviving Son

WILLFUL SUBMISSION OF FALSE INFORMATION IS A VIOLATION OF THE LAW AND, UPON CONVICTION, IS PUNISHABLE BY IMPRISONMENT FOR UP TO FIVE YEARS OR A FINE OF NOT MORE THAN $250,000, OR BOTH.

10. I certify that the information I have provided on this form is true, accurate and complete to the best of my knowledge and belief.

_____
(Signature of Registrant)

_____
(Date)

SSS Form 9 (APR 88)   Previous editions are obsolete. Stock will be destroyed.   OMB Approval: 3240-0008

APPENDIX III: SSS FORM 9

SELECTIVE SERVICE SYSTEM
CLAIM DOCUMENTATION FORM CONSCIENTIOUS OBJECTOR
(RIPS/RIMS)

Date Issued	Complete and Return Not Later than
Registrant's Selective Service No. Full Name Complete Address	Local Board No. Area Office Address

⌐   ⌐

└   └

INSTRUCTIONS TO REGISTRANT: The purpose of this form is to help you provide the information needed by your Local Board to determine if you qualify for reclassification as a Conscientious Objector. Your objection may be based on religious, moral or ethical beliefs, or a combination of these beliefs.

Before you prepare the information requested on this form, we recommend that you read the Conscientious Objector section of the Information for Registrants Booklet, which is available at your U.S. Post Office or Selective Service System Area Office. You must complete this form, attach your statement (Part II) to the form, and mail or deliver it to your Area Office no later than the return date shown above or your claim will not be considered. You may also attach letters from persons who have personal knowledge of your conscientious objection.

You will be required to appear before your Local Board at the time it considers your claim..

PART I

Check the box in this part that pertains to your claim.

1. ☐ I claim exemption only from training and service as a combatant member of the Armed Forces (Class 1-A-O).

   (To qualify, you must establish to the satisfaction of the Board that you are conscientiously opposed to participation in combatant military training and service in any war, based on deeply held moral, ethical or religious beliefs.)

2. ☐ I claim exemption from all training and service as a member of the Armed Forces (Class 1-O).

   (To qualify, you must establish to the satisfaction of the Board that you are conscientiously opposed to participation in combatant and noncombatant military training and service in any war, based on deeply held moral, ethical or religious beliefs.)

(Continued on reverse)

SSS FORM 22 (AUG 2000) OMB APPROVAL 3240-0028

11-8

APPENDIX IV: SSS FORM 22 FRONT PAGE

PART II

Prepare and attach written responses to the information requested below. If you wish, you may attach letters from persons who know you and are familiar with your beliefs. You may also attach any other pertinent information you would like the Local Board to consider.

1. Describe your beliefs which are the reasons for you claiming conscientious objection to combatant military training and service or to all military training and service.

2. Describe how and when you acquired these beliefs. Your answer may include such information as the influence of family members or other persons; training, if applicable; your personal experiences; membership in organizations; books and readings which influenced you.

3. Explain what most clearly shows that your beliefs are deeply held. You may wish to include a description of how your beliefs affect the way you live.

PART III

List below, the names of individuals and organizations whose letters or documents (papers) you are submitting with this form to insure that all letters or documents have been received.

PART IV   REGISTRANT CERTIFICATE

I certify that all information I have provided on this form and other documents that I am submitting to support this claim are true, accurate and complete to the best of my knowledge and belief.

_____   _____
(Signature of Registrant)   (Date)

WILLFUL SUBMISSION OF FALSE INFORMATION IS A VIOLATION OF LAW AND, UPON CONVICTION, IS PUNISHABLE BY IMPRISONMENT FOR UP TO FIVE YEARS OR A FINE OF NOT MORE THAN $250,000, OR BOTH.

PRIVACY ACT STATEMENT

The Military Selective Service Act and Selective Service Regulations authorizes the Selective Service System to receive the information requested on this form. However, you are not required to provide that information.

The principal use of the requested information is to assist the Selective Service to adjudicate your claim for postponement and/or reclassification promptly and equitably. This information may be furnished to the following agencies for the purposes indicated:

Department of Justice - to review and process suspected violations of the Military Selective Service Act and to litigate civil actions occurring under or incident to the Military Selective Service Act.

Federal Bureau of Investigation - to locate an individual suspected of violation of the Military Selective Service Act.

Immigration and Naturalization Service - to provide information for use in determining an individual's eligibility for reentry into the United States and for United States citizenship.

Department of State - for determination of an alien's eligibility for possible entry into the United States and United States citizenship.

Department of Health and Human Services - to locate parents pursuant to the Child Support Enforcement Act (42 U.S.C. 651 et seq).

Your failure to provide the requested information may result in denial of your claim for postponement and/or reclassification because of insufficient information.

SSS FORM 22 (AUG 2000) OMB APPROVAL 3240-0028

11-9

APPENDIX V: FORM 22 BACK PAGE

SELECTIVE SERVICE SYSTEM
NOTICE OF CLASSIFICATION
(RIPS/RIMS)

Date of Mailing:

Registrant's Selective Service No. Full Name, Complete Address

Office Identification and Address

PART I. SUMMARY OF CLASSIFICATION ACTION

1 Classifications	2 Decisions		3 Not Considered	4 Classified By				5 Board Vote		6 Reason(s) for Denial
	a Grant	b Deny		a AO	b LB	c DAB	d NAB	a Grant	b Deny	
☐ 1-A-O										
☐ 1-O										
☐ 1-O-S										
☐ 2-D										
☐ 3-A										
☐ 3-A-S										
☐ 4-D										
☐ 1-D-D										
☐ 4-B										
☐ 4-C										
☐ 4-G										
☐ 4-A										
☐ 4-A-A										
☐ 4-W										
☐ 1-D-E										
☐ 1-C										
☐ 1-W										
☐ 4-T										

PART II.   YOUR PRESENT CLASSIFICATION IS: _____

Expiration Date (if applicable): _____

PART III.   REQUEST FOR REVIEW OR APPEAL

☐   I hereby request a review/appeal of the denial(s) of my classification claim(s) as shown on this form

☐   I also request a personal appearance before the local/appeal board at the time it considers my claim. I understand I must pay for any travel expenses incurred in connection with this appearance.

_____
(SIGNATURE OF REGISTRANT)

_____
(DATE)

SSS FORM 110 (AUG 2000)   COPY 2 - REGISTRANT

11-39

APPENDIX VI: SSS FORM 110

Local Board/Area Office
Street Address
City, State, ZIP

SELECTIVE SERVICE SYSTEM
ORDER TO PERFORM ALTERNATIVE SERVICE
(RIPS/RIMS)

Date of Issuance:

Registrant's Name and SSN	Social Security Number
Street Address	Random Sequence Number
City, State, Zip	

This is your Order to Perform Alternative Service in lieu of induction into the Armed Forces of the United States.

You have been reclassified 1-W (Conscientious Objector ordered to perform alternative service). Under the authority of the Military Selective Service Act you are ordered to perform alternative service for ____ consecutive months, to begin on the date to be determined by the Director.

Your performance of alternative service will be monitored by the Alternative Service Office (ASO) located at: _____, which will contact you in the near future to schedule a job counseling session and assist you in locating a suitable job. During your performance of alternative service, any contact with the Selective Service System should be with the ASO having jurisdictional responsibility for you.

Enclosed is an Alternative Service Worker Guide, which provides general information about the type of work you will perform. Also enclosed is a Skills Questionnaire (SSS Form 156) which asks for information to assist the ASO in placing you in an alternative service job. Please complete and return the SSS Form 156 as soon as your job counseling session is scheduled.

If you are a student pursuing a full-time course of instruction at a high school, college or similar institution of learning, have the enclosed SSS Form 109 (Student Certificate) completed and signed by an authorized school official. The SSS Form 109 must be returned to the Area Office shown above within 10 days from the date of this Order.

_____
(SIGNATURE)   LOCAL BOARD MEMBER

_____
PRINTED NAME

Warning: If you fail to follow the directions in this Order, you may be reported as a suspected violator of the Military Selective Service Act and, if convicted, be subject to imprisonment for up to five years, a fine of up to $250,000, or both.

SSS FORM 155 (AUG 2000)   ORIGINAL

11-60

APPENDIX VII: SSS FORM 152

Local Board/Area Office
Street Address
City, State, ZIP

SELECTIVE SERVICE SYSTEM
ORDER TO PERFORM ALTERNATIVE SERVICE
(RIPS/RIMS)

Date of Issuance:

Registrant's Name and SSN   Social Security Number
Street Address   Random Sequence Number
City, State, Zip

This is your Order to Perform Alternative Service in lieu of induction into the Armed Forces of the United States.

You have been reclassified 1-W (Conscientious Objector ordered to perform alternative service). Under the authority of the Military Selective Service Act you are ordered to perform alternative service for ____ consecutive months, to begin on the date to be determined by the Director.

Your performance of alternative service will be monitored by the Alternative Service Office (ASO) located at: _____, which will contact you in the near future to schedule a job counseling session and assist you in locating a suitable job. During your performance of alternative service, any contact with the Selective Service System should be with the ASO having jurisdictional responsibility for you.

Enclosed is an Alternative Service Worker Guide, which provides general information about the type of work you will perform. Also enclosed is a Skills Questionnaire (SSS Form 156) which asks for information to assist the ASO in placing you in an alternative service job. Please complete and return the SSS Form 156 as soon as your job counseling session is scheduled.

If you are a student pursuing a full-time course of instruction at a high school, college or similar institution of learning, have the enclosed SSS Form 109 (Student Certificate) completed and signed by an authorized school official. The SSS Form 109 must be returned to the Area Office shown above within 10 days from the date of this Order.

_____
(SIGNATURE)   LOCAL BOARD MEMBER

_____
PRINTED NAME

Warning: If you fail to follow the directions in this Order, you may be reported as a suspected violator of the Military Selective Service Act and, if convicted, be subject to imprisonment for up to five years, a fine of up to $250,000, or both.

SSS FORM 155 (AUG 2000)   ORIGINAL

11-60

APPENDIX VIII: SSS FORM 155

Local Board/Area Office
Street Address
City, State, ZIP

SELECTIVE SERVICE SYSTEM
ORDER TO REPORT FOR ARMED FORCES EXAMINATION
(RIPS)

Date of Issuance

Registrant's Name   Selective Service Number
Street Address   Social Security Number
City, State, Zip   Random Sequence Number

This is your Order to report for and submit to an Armed Forces Examination for the purpose of determining your potential acceptability for military service.

You are hereby directed to report, with this Order, to:_____
                                                      (DESIGNATED ASSEMBLY POINT)
on _____ at _____ for transportation to the Military Entrance Processing Station (MEPS)
      (DATE)   (TIME)
in _____
            (CITY AND STATE)

Upon completion of your examination, you will be returned to the place of reporting shown above.

If you are closer to the MEPS than to the place you are ordered to report, and if you wish to go directly to the MEPS, contact the Area Office shown above for instructions.

If you are so far from your Area Office that reporting in compliance with this Order would be a hardship, and if you wish to report to the Area Office where you are now located, contact that Area Office and request a transfer for examination.

You will be furnished transportation, and meals and lodging when necessary, from the designated place of reporting to the MEPS and return. It is possible that you may be retained at the MEPS for more than one day for the purpose of further processing. If you have any physical or mental condition which you believe may disqualify you for service, or if you are physically incapable of reporting to the MEPS, contact your Area Office for instructions.

If you believe you qualify for a postponement of your examination, complete the attached Request for Postponement of Armed Forces Examination (SSS Form 233P) and return it to your Area Office before the date you are scheduled to report.

Read the Important Information Sheet provided with this Order. If you fail to obey this Order you may be reported as a suspected violator of the Military Selective Service Act and, if convicted, subject to imprisonment for up to five years, a fine of up to $250,000, or both.

Director of Selective Service

Attachment

FOR INFORMATION AND ADVICE, CONTACT ANY SELECTIVE SERVICE AREA OFFICE

SSS FORM 233

11-105

APPENDIX IX: SSS FORM 233

AND THE UNITED STATES ARMED FORCES

SELECTIVE SERVICE SYSTEM
REQUEST FOR POSTPONEMENT OF ARMED FORCES EXAMINATION
(RIPS)

Date of Issuance

Registrant's Name	Selective Service Number
Street Address	Social Security Number
City, State, Zip	Random Sequence Number

(MAKE ANY NECESSARY ADDRESS CORRECTIONS ABOVE)

I request a postponement of my Armed Forces examination for the reason(s) checked below:

_____ My injury or illness

_____ Death in my immediate family

_____ Emergency beyond my control (Describe)

_____

_____

_____ Religious holiday which I normally observe
Name of holiday:_____
Date holiday begins:_____
Date holiday ends:_____

_____ Scheduled for state or national board licensing/certification examination, required before I can practice my
profession or occupation
Name of examination:_____
Date of examination: _____

I expect the condition on which this request is based to end on or about: _____ .
(DATE)

_____   _____
(SIGNATURE OF REGISTRANT)   (DATE)

As an individual who is conscientiously opposed to both combatant and noncombatant military training and service,
I hereby request consideration for conscientious objector status and wish to have my Armed Forces examination waived
until a decision is made on my claim for Class 1-O. I understand receiving this waiver will prohibit me from filing a
claim for any other class and if my 1-O claim is denied I will be rescheduled for examination. I further understand that
if my claim for Class 1-O is granted, I will not be given another opportunity to undergo an Armed Forces examination.

_____   _____
(SIGNATURE OF REGISTRANT)   (DATE)

SSS FORM 233P

11-108

APPENDIX X: SSS FORM 233P

SELECTIVE SERVICE SYSTEM

NORTH SUBURBAN, IL 60197

▶ REGISTRANT'S NAME
STREET ADDRESS
CITY, STATE, ZIP

ORDER TO REPORT FOR INDUCTION

DATE
SEL. SER. NO.   INDUCTION ORDER NO.
SOC. SEC. NO.   LOCAL BOARD NO.
RSN   STATE CODE

THIS IS YOUR ORDER TO REPORT FOR AND SUBMIT TO EXAMINATION AND
INDUCTION INTO THE ARMED FORCES OF THE UNITED STATES. BY DIRECTION
OF THE PRESIDENT, YOU HAVE BEEN CLASSIFIED 1-A (AVAILABLE FOR
UNRESTRICTED MILITARY SERVICE) AND ARE DIRECTED TO REPORT, WITH THIS
ORDER, TO THE MILITARY ENTRANCE PROCESSING STATION (MEPS) LOCATED AT:
                         (ADDRESS)
ON: (DATE)   AT: (TIME)

YOU MAY REPORT TO ANOTHER MEPS IF IT IS CLOSER TO WHERE YOU ARE NOW.
MEPS ADDRESSES MAY BE OBTAINED FROM ANY SELECTIVE SERVICE AREA
OFFICE, ARMED FORCES RECRUITING OFFICE OR MILITARY INSTALLATION.

IF YOU ARE FOUND QUALIFIED FOR MILITARY SERVICE, YOU WILL BE INDUCTED
IMMEDIATELY INTO THE ARMED FORCES AND GO DIRECTLY TO TRAINING. WHEN
YOU ARE INDUCTED, YOU WILL BE RECLASSIFIED 1-C (MEMBER OF THE ARMED
FORCES). IF YOU ARE NOT INDUCTED, YOU WILL BE SENT HOME.

IF YOU BELIEVE YOU QUALIFY FOR A RECLASSIFICATION OR A POSTPONEMENT
OF INDUCTION, CONTACT THE SELECTIVE SERVICE AREA OFFICE LOCATED AT:
                         (ADDRESS)
                         (ADDRESS)
PRIOR TO THE DATE YOU ARE TO REPORT FOR INDUCTION. SEE PAGE 2.

THE TRAVEL WARRANT ENCLOSED IS TO BE USED ONLY BY YOU FOR YOUR
TRANSPORTATION TO THE MEPS. IF NO TRANSPORTATAION IS AVAILABLE,
CONTACT THE AREA OFFICE LISTED ABOVE IMMEDIATELY.

READ THE IMPORTANT INFORMATION PROVIDED WITH THIS ORDER. IF YOU
FAIL TO OBEY THIS ORDER, YOU MAY BE REPORTED AS A SUSPECTED VIOLATOR
OF THE MILITARY SELECTIVE SERVICE ACT AND, IF CONVICTED, SUBJECT TO
IMPRISONMENT FOR UP TO FIVE YEARS, A FINE OF UP TO $250,000, OR BOTH.

BY DIRECTION OF THE PRESIDENT:
                                    DIRECTOR OF SELECTIVE SERVICE

SSS FORM 252

TO REPLY BY MAILGRAM MESSAGE, SEE REVERSE SIDE FOR WESTERN UNION'S TOLL - FREE PHONE NUMBERS

RIMS   JUNE 1988
                        11-127

APPENDIX XI: Form 252 FRONT

PAGE 2

► HOW TO TRAVEL TO MEPS

TAKE THE ATTACHED TRAVEL WARRANT TO A BUS OR TRAIN TICKET AGENT WHO
WILL ISSUE YOU A TICKET TO THE CITY WHERE THE MEPS IS LOCATED. WHEN
YOU ARRIVE IN THAT CITY ASK THE AGENT FOR DIRECTIONS TO THE MEPS.
IF YOU COME BY CAR, ARRANGE TO HAVE IT RETURNED HOME. RESIDENTS OF
ALASKA AND ITS OFFSHORE ISLANDS ARE AUTHORIZED TO TRAVEL BY LAND, SEA
OR AIR. IF YOU MUST BUY YOUR OWN TICKET YOU MAY CLAIM PAYMENT AT THE
MEPS WHEN YOU TURN IN YOUR RECEIPTS AND UNUSED TRAVEL WARRANT. THE
PAYMENT WILL BE SENT TO YOU AS SOON AS POSSIBLE. YOU ARE STRONGLY
ENCOURAGED TO USE THE TRAVEL WARRANT AND NOT TRAVEL BY CAR.

WHAT TO BRING

COMFORTABLE CLOTHING AND TOILET ARTICLES FOR THREE DAYS WHICH CAN BE
CONTAINED IN A TRAVEL BAG NO LARGER THAN 9" X 13" X 24" AND ALL OF
THE FOLLOWING THAT APPLY TO YOU: BIRTH CERTIFICATE, SOCIAL SECURITY
CARD, DRIVER'S LICENSE, LAST SCHOOL RECORD, DOCTOR'S STATEMENT AND
HOSPITAL RECORDS IF YOU HAVE A HISTORY OF PHYSICAL OR MENTAL
DISORDER, EYEGLASSES OR CONTACT LENSES, PRESCRIPTION DRUGS YOU TAKE,
RECORDS OF COURT DECISIONS THAT AFFECT YOUR STATUS, PROOF OF MARITAL
STATUS IF OTHER THAN SINGLE, CHILDREN'S BIRTH CERTIFICATES, PRIOR
MILITARY SERVICE RECORD (DD FORM 124). DO NOT BRING FAMILY, FRIENDS,
PETS, WEAPONS/KNIVES, NONPRESCRIPTION DRUGS, LARGE SUMS OF MONEY OR
EXPENSIVE JEWELRY.

ATTENTION ALIENS

IF YOU ARE AN ALIEN AND HAVE LIVED IN THE UNITED STATES FOR LESS THAN
ONE YEAR, THIS IS YOUR ORDER TO FURNISH PROOF OF YOUR STATUS. SEND
THE PROOF TO THE AREA OFFICE SHOWN ON THIS ORDER WITHIN TEN DAYS FROM
THE DATE THE ORDER WAS ISSUED AND DO NOT GO TO THE MEPS. IF YOU HAVE
LIVED IN THE UNITED STATES OVER ONE YEAR, DISREGARD THIS PARAGRAPH.

POSTPONEMENT AND RECLASSIFICATION INFORMATION

YOU MAY FILE A CLAIM FOR POSTPONEMENT OR RECLASSIFICATION AT ANY TIME
PRIOR TO THE DATE YOU ARE SCHEDULED TO REPORT FOR INDUCTION.
INFORMATION IS AVAILABLE FROM ANY SELECTIVE SERVICE AREA OFFICE, OR
THROUGH INFORMATION BOOKLETS FURNISHED FOR REGISTRANTS AT ALL U.S.
POST OFFICES, CONSULATES AND EMBASSIES. DO NOT REPORT TO THE MEPS
AFTER YOU HAVE FILED A CLAIM IN WRITING WITH YOUR AREA OFFICE. YOU
WILL BE ADVISED BY THE AREA OFFICE OF ADDITIONAL INFORMATION YOU
NEED TO PROVIDE IN SUPPORT OF YOUR CLAIM, AND THE PROCEDURES TO BE
FOLLOWED FOR SUBMITTING DOCUMENTATION.

TO REPLY BY MAILGRAM MESSAGE, SEE REVERSE SIDE FOR WESTERN UNION'S TOLL - FREE PHONE NUMBERS

RIMS   JUNE 1988
                              11-128

APPENDIX XII: SSS Form 252 back

Local Board/Area office
Street Address
City, State, ZIP

SELECTIVE SERVICE SYSTEM
ORDER TO REPORT FOR INDUCTION
(RIPS)

Date of Issuance

Registrant's Name   Selective Service Number
Street Address   Social Security Number
City, State, Zip   Random Sequence Number

This is your Order to report for and submit to induction into the Armed Forces of the United States. You are hereby directed to report, with this Order, to:

_____ on _____ at _____ for transportation to the
     (DESIGNATED ASSEMBLY POINT)   (DATE)   (TIME)
Military Entrance Processing Station (MEPS) in _____ for induction into the
                          (CITY & STATE)
Armed Forces.

If you are closer to the MEPS than to the place you are ordered to report, and if you wish to go directly to the MEPS, contact the Area Office shown above for instructions. Do not plan to travel by privately-owned vehicle unless you make arrangements to have the vehicle returned home.

If you are so far from your Area Office that reporting in compliance with this Order would be a hardship, and if you wish to report to the Area Office where you are now located, contact that Area Office and request a transfer for induction.

You will be furnished transportation, and meals and lodging where necessary, from the designated place of reporting to the MEPS. When you are inducted, you will be administratively reclassified 1-C (Member of the Armed Forces).

If you are a full-time student, if you are scheduled to enter one of the U.S. service academies, or if you have been accepted for certain ROTC programs, you may qualify for a postponement of induction. You may also ask for a postponement if you are scheduled to take a state or national licensing examination, or if your induction is scheduled for the same day as a religious holiday you normally observe. If any of these conditions apply to you, complete the attached Request for Postponement of Induction (SSS Form 262P) and return it to your Area Office prior to the day you are scheduled to report.

Read the Important Information Sheet provided with this Order. If you fail to obey this Order, you may be reported as a suspected violator of the Military Selective Service Act and, if convicted, subject to imprisonment for up to five years, a fine of up to $250,000, or both.

DIRECTOR OF SELECTIVE SERVICE

FOR INFORMATION AND ADVICE, CONTACT ANY SELECTIVE SERVICE OFFICE

SSS FORM 262

11-115

APPENDIX XIII: SSS FORM 262

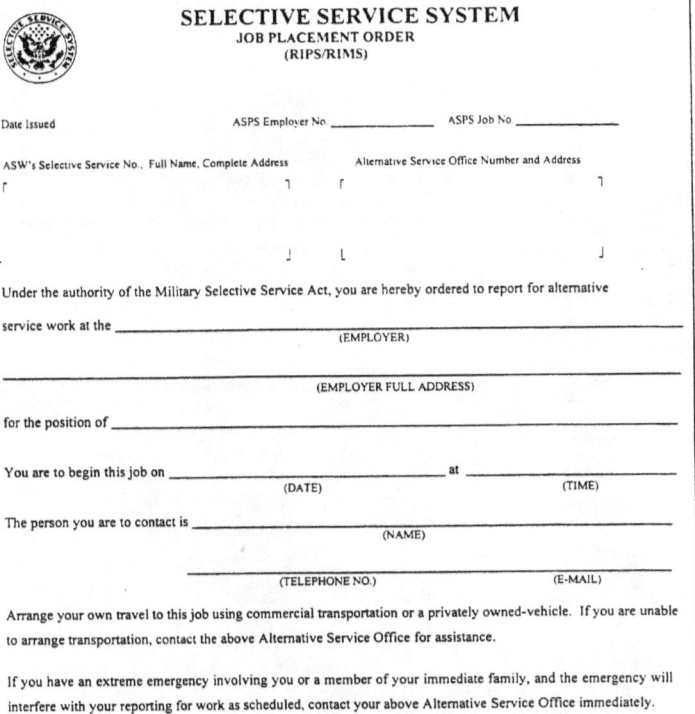

SELECTIVE SERVICE SYSTEM
JOB PLACEMENT ORDER
(RIPS/RIMS)

Date Issued   ASPS Employer No _____   ASPS Job No _____

ASW's Selective Service No., Full Name, Complete Address   Alternative Service Office Number and Address

Under the authority of the Military Selective Service Act, you are hereby ordered to report for alternative

service work at the _____
(EMPLOYER)

_____
(EMPLOYER FULL ADDRESS)

for the position of _____

You are to begin this job on _____ at _____
                              (DATE)   (TIME)

The person you are to contact is _____
                                          (NAME)

_____
(TELEPHONE NO.)   (E-MAIL)

Arrange your own travel to this job using commercial transportation or a privately owned-vehicle. If you are unable to arrange transportation, contact the above Alternative Service Office for assistance.

If you have an extreme emergency involving you or a member of your immediate family, and the emergency will interfere with your reporting for work as scheduled, contact your above Alternative Service Office immediately.

If you are granted a postponement of your reporting date and that postponement is not acceptable to the employer, you will be ordered to report for a new job counseling session or interview at the end of your postponement.

_____
(ALTERNATIVE SERVICE OFFICE SUPERVISOR)

WARNING: If you disobey this Order, you are subject, upon conviction, to imprisonment for up to 5 years or a fine of not more than $250,000, or both, for violation of the Military Selective Service Act.

SSS FORM 162 (AUG 2000)   (Circle Copy) ORIGINAL - ASW, COPY 1 - 101A

11-79

APPENDIX XIV: SSS FORM 162

Circle the appropriate copy designator

Copy 1   Copy 2   Copy 3   Copy 4

PERSONNEL ACTION

For use of this form, see AR 600-8-6 and DA PAM 600-8-21; the proponent agency is ODCSPER

DATA REQUIRED BY THE PRIVACY ACT OF 1974

AUTHORITY: Title 5, Section 3012; Title 10, USC, E.O. 9397.

PRINCIPAL PURPOSE: Used by soldier in accordance with DA PAM 600-8-21 when requesting a personnel action on his/her own behalf (Section III).

ROUTINE USES: To initiate the processing of a personnel action being requested by the soldier.

DISCLOSURE: Voluntary. Failure to provide social security number may result in a delay or error in processing of the request for personnel action.

1. THRU (Include ZIP Code)	2. TO (Include ZIP Code)	3. FROM (Include ZIP Code)

SECTION I - PERSONAL IDENTIFICATION

4. NAME (Last, First, MI) NAME	5. GRADE OR RANK/PMOS/AOC	6. SOCIAL SECURITY NUMBER

SECTION II - DUTY STATUS CHANGE (AR 600-8-6)

7. The above soldier's duty status is changed from _____ to

_____ effective _____ hours, _____

SECTION III - REQUEST FOR PERSONNEL ACTION

8. I request the following action: (Check as appropriate)

Service School (Enl only)	Special Forces Training/Assignment	Identification Card
ROTC or Reserve Component Duty	On-the-Job Training (Enl only)	Identification Tags
Volunteering For Oversea Service	Retesting in Army Personnel Tests	Separate Rations
Ranger Training	Reassignment Married Army Couples	Leave - Excess/Advance/Outside CONUS
Reassignment Extreme Family Problems	X Reclassification to 1-0 Status	Change of Name/SSN/DOB
Exchange Reassignment (Enl only)	Officer Candidate School	X Other (Specify) DISCHARGE AS A
Airborne Training	Asgmt of Pers with Exceptional Family Members	CONSCIENTIOUS OBJECTOR

9. SIGNATURE OF SOLDIER (When required)	10. DATE (YYYYMMDD)

SECTION IV - REMARKS (Applies to Sections II, III, and V) (Continue on separate sheet)

SECTION V - CERTIFICATION/APPROVAL/DISAPPROVAL

11. I certify that the duty status change (Section II) or that the request for personnel action (Section III) contained herein -

☐ HAS BEEN VERIFIED ☐ RECOMMEND APPROVAL ☐ RECOMMEND DISAPPROVAL ☐ IS APPROVED ☐ IS DISAPPROVED

12. COMMANDER/AUTHORIZED REPRESENTATIVE	13. SIGNATURE	14. DATE (YYYYMMDD)

DA FORM 4187, JAN 2000   PREVIOUS EDITIONS ARE OBSOLETE   USAPA V1.00

APPENDIX XV: FORM DA 4187

SEPARATION REQUEST FORM
(For use of this form see USAREC Reg 601-56)

TYPES OF SEPARATION

Check one box only:

[x] VOLUNTARY

[ ] INVOLUNTARY

Check one box only:

[ ] RA DELAYED STATUS
[x] DEP
[ ] FRAUDULENT, ERRONEOUS, OR DEFECTIVE ENLISTMENT
[ ] USAR DEP

Last Name, First Name, Middle Initial	SSN			
Adair, Yolanda M.	012-34-5678			

Street Address	City	State	Telephone Number
2010 Hardknock Lane	Experience	MO	(314) 436-1234

DEP DATA

DEP-In Date	PADD	Recruiter/RSID	AFQT/Education
29 Jan 96	27 Mar 96	Lyons/5J1K	79/126

Unit	Street Address	City, State, and ZIP Code	Telephone Number

REASON FOR SEPARATION OR VOID ENLISTMENT

[ ] Apathy or Personal Problems
[ ] Failure to Graduate
[ ] Hardship
[ ] Dependency
[ ] Marriage
[ ] Failure to Report
[ ] Moral (Non-EPTS)
[ ] Refused to Enlist
[ ] Lost Original Option Declines Alternate
[x] Higher Education w/wo Scholarship

[ ] Concealed Medical (EPTS)
[ ] Concealed Dependents
[ ] Concealed Prior Service
[ ] Concealed Moral (EPTS)
[ ] Ringer
[ ] Other

Applicant Interested In:

[ ] Army Reserve
[ ] Army National Guard
[ ] Reapplying for Army

Remarks

Date	Signature of Individual
6 Mar 96	/signed/
Date	Typed Name and Grade of Guidance Counselor or Recruiter
6 Mar 96	James A. Bracken, SFC
Date	Signature of Guidance Counselor or Recruiter
6 Mar 96	/signed/

USAREC Fm 986, 1 Jul 89

Figure 3-1. Sample of a completed USAREC Fm 986

UPDATE • USAREC Reg 601-56   27

APPENDIX XVI: FORM 986

DEPARTMENT OF THE ARMY
U.S. Army Recruiting Battalion Fort Knox
1307 Third Avenue
Fort Knox, Kentucky 40121-2726

ORDER 12-1   12 January 1997

JONES, Allen J., 001-00-9999, SGT/E-5, (WO6QAA), 1000 Main St., Anywhere, KY 00033

You are separated from component indicated.

Authority: AR 135-178

Effective Date: 4 January 1997 (VOCO Confirmed)

Component: USAR DELAYED ENTRY PROGRAM, FORT KNOX, KY 40121

Additional Instructions: N/A

FOR ARMY USE:
HOR: Anywhere, KY 00033
Format: 500

/s/ signed
J.J. SMITH
LTC, FA
Commanding

DISTRIBUTION:
1-JONES, Allen J., 1000 Main St., Anywhere, KY 00033
1-Rctg Bn Record Set
1-Rctg Bn DEP Separation Record Copy (MPRJ)
1-Fort Knox MEPS, 101 Main St., Anywhere, KY 00033
1-Cdr, ARPERCEN, ATTN: ARPC-PRA-R, 9700 Page Blvd., St. Louis, MO 63132-5200

Figure G-2. Sample Order Format 500

APPENDIX XVII: Sample Discharge

DODI 1336.1, January 6, 1989

E1. *ENCLOSURE 1*

CAUTION: NOT TO BE USED FOR IDENTIFICATION PURPOSES

THIS IS AN IMPORTANT RECORD. SAFEGUARD IT.

ANY ALTERATIONS IN SHADED AREAS RENDER FORM VOID

CERTIFICATE OF RELEASE OR DISCHARGE FROM ACTIVE DUTY

DD FORM 214, FEB 2000 — PREVIOUS EDITION IS OBSOLETE. — MEMBER - 1

13

APPENDIX XVIII: FORM DD 214

www.ingramcontent.com/pod-product-compliance
Lightning Source LLC
Chambersburg PA
CBHW021004180526
45163CB00005B/1887